Denine

One Mother's Journey With A Profoundly Handicapped Child

To Bill
May God meet with you
as you read our story
Chris Forster

Chris Czarnata Forster

 FriesenPress

Suite 300 - 990 Fort St
Victoria, BC, V8V 3K2
Canada

www.friesenpress.com

Copyright © 2017 by Chris Czarnata Forster
First Edition — 2017

All rights reserved.

No part of this publication may be reproduced in any form, or by any means, electronic or mechanical, including photocopying, recording, or any information browsing, storage, or retrieval system, without permission in writing from FriesenPress.

ISBN
978-1-4602-7515-3 (Hardcover)
978-1-4602-7516-0 (Paperback)
978-1-4602-7517-7 (eBook)

1. BIOGRAPHY & AUTOBIOGRAPHY, PERSONAL MEMOIRS

Distributed to the trade by The Ingram Book Company

Table of Contents

v	Dedication
ix	Foreword
1	*Chapter* 1: Denine Kamillia
7	*Chapter* 2: My Family of Origin
13	*Chapter* 3: Why is She So Stiff?
21	*Chapter* 4: More Tests
27	*Chapter* 5: Home Again
35	*Chapter* 6: Cerebral Palsy Centre
41	*Chapter* 7: Coping
49	*Chapter* 8: High Fever
55	*Chapter* 9: Daniel Kenneth
61	*Chapter* 10: Dirty Dishes & Diapers
69	*Chapter* 11: Depression
77	*Chapter* 12: Vacation at Last
83	*Chapter* 13: Angel Unaware
87	*Chapter* 14: Surgery
93	*Chapter* 15: Child Development Centre
95	*Chapter* 16: I Want Another Baby

101	*Chapter* 17: Can't You Help Me?
109	*Chapter* 18: Can We Pray With You?
115	*Chapter* 19: Melanie Crystal
121	*Chapter* 20: I Didn't Know!
127	*Chapter* 21: Placement
135	*Chapter* 22: Dealing With Death
145	*Chapter* 23: "Lord Change Me"
149	*Chapter* 24: Peace in My Heart
153	*Chapter* 25: Victory in Jesus
159	*Chapter* 26: Life After Denine
165	Epilogue
167	Some Final Thoughts

Dedication

This book is dedicated to our two children Daniel and Melanie who were too young to remember the sister who had such an impact on our lives.

It was a strange day all around
It was very windy
But not too cold
Sunday, April 1, 1979
The phone call came before breakfast
I was still in bed

Denine was having trouble breathing
They sent her to the hospital
The ambulance siren wailed in the background
This was for real!

How many times in those five years
Had I gone to see her in a hospital?
St. Joseph's
The General
McMaster
Chedoke
Toronto Sick Children's

What were the reasons?
Tests
Flu
Pneumonia
More tests
Emergency treatment for dehydration
Surgery on her legs
Double pneumonia
Plastic surgery
X-rays
High fevers

How many high fevers had she run?
Did they ever find the cause?

How many doctors had we seen?
Therapists
Nurses
Lab technicians

How many hours had we spent waiting?
Waiting to see doctors
Waiting for the medication to start working
Waiting for the fever to go down
Waiting for the crying to stop
Waiting for other people to drive when I could not

Then waiting with a two year old boy
Running around
Climbing all over me
And everything else
Demanding a drink
Trips to the bathroom
Then I was pregnant again
And my back hurt so much

How I hated to wait
Maybe hate is too nice a word for what I felt
Those inconsiderate people
Didn't they know I had an appointment at eleven a.m.?
And now it's 12:35

Where was my husband in those days?
At home farming
Fourteen hours a day
Seven days a week
365 days a year
In those first eight years of our marriage
We went on vacation once

And yet God never left our side
He was always there when I needed Him
How many times did I cry out to Him?
In those days of sickness
In those nights of fever
In those hours of waiting
He was always right there
But I didn't know
Until after I had stopped fighting
Until after I had accepted

God had chosen ME
He had chosen me
Out of all the mothers I know
He had chosen me
To be the mother of a very special child
A profoundly handicapped child
Denine
This is our story

Foreword

Tears flowed as I read *Denine*. I was flooded with memories and realized that meeting Chris and Ken Forster was the Divine intersection of two stories. It is humbling and faith inspiring for me to write this forward. I am reminded that Jesus brings His life and healing into our pain and sorrow.

My husband, Terry, and I were at the beginning of our adventure. Newly married in May of that year, we moved into the village church manse. I was twenty years old and Terry was twenty three. We had so little life experience but we loved Jesus and wanted to serve Him and share how much He loved people. We were about to be immersed in more "life" than we had imagined.

The next few months were spent setting up our first home, visiting people and exploring the new role of the "Minister and his wife". We had visits with Chris and Ken at their house and they visited our house. I remember one of the first visits,

Chris, Ken and Daniel stopped by the manse after church. It was lunch-time. Growing up as a Pastor's kid, for me, Sunday lunch was a roast beef dinner. I quickly grabbed a roast from the freezer, threw it into the oven and announced that dinner would be ready in a couple of hours. Chris laughed and looked at Ken; Ken said "Do you have any bread? We could have sandwiches." There was no feeling of expectation or performance about them and I was instantly drawn to them and to their young son Daniel. Daniel was precocious, defiant, rambunctious and completely undisciplined (so I thought). He had just turned three. I did not have children but I was sure that Daniel needed to be reined in. Chris was very pregnant and seemed too tired or heavy to deal with Daniel and nothing seemed to bother Ken. Over the course of subsequent visits, Chris talked about her older daughter, Denine. As I listened, I realized that there was so much more to their story than what I could see on the surface.

Denine was profoundly disabled and in a Home recovering from a bed sore. Chris talked about life with Denine. I was very curious and asked lots of questions. A few years earlier, I had volunteered at the London's Children's Psychiatric Institute. I was currently in university studying Child Psychology. I was hoping to work with children who had special needs, but I had never met the mother of a child with severe disabilities.

One day Chris asked me if I wanted to go with her to visit Denine. My response was an instant "yes", but inside I was very nervous. How would I feel knowing that this child belonged to my friend? How did she feel about being her mother? Would I say the right thing? I was the minister's wife; I must say the right thing. Chris and I walked together into the hospital-like room at the Home. There was a small child lying in the crib on the other side of the room. She was long, very thin and stiff. Her hair was thick and dark brown. The skin on her face was tight. I couldn't tell if she was crying or just vocalizing, but she seemed to know her mother was there. Chris proudly introduced me to her daughter. Gently stroking Denine's hair, Chris talked to me about her and why she was in the home. I saw such love in Chris's eyes, tenderness in her voice and a desire for me to know Denine. I was in awe of this mother's love and very aware of her pain. I didn't have many words to say. In fact, I couldn't remember what I said until Chris told me years later.

Denine died not many months after that visit. Her funeral was the first child my husband had to bury. The morning Chris called to tell us that Denine was gone, I had a vision of Denine, healthy and beautiful, walking boldly up to Jesus. What joy to be so vividly reminded that there is life after death, that Denine was safe in the arms of a loving Saviour.

In any ministry there are always people who disagree with the Gospel of Jesus and over the course of our first year at the church, tensions rose and the stress became unbearable. Terry and I were both in full-time university, as well as trying to fulfill our increasing duties and the expectations at the church. The stresses eventually reached a climax and we decided that we did not "need to live in this conflict"!

We climbed into our car and headed to Hamilton to look for apartments. As we cried out to God, in the midst of our frustration, grief and anxiety, we heard that still small voice saying, "Are you willing to stay on this path for the Forster's?" The question was accompanied by God's heart of love for this family. Tears flowed as we both answered, "Yes". We drove in silence, but with new resolve, back to the two little churches in the farming village.

Chris and I continued to spend time together when I wasn't studying or attending classes. There was a hunger in Chris for something or someone bigger than herself. I just kept pointing her to Jesus. She kept asking questions. We prayed, read the Bible, and grew together. By the time Terry and I graduated and moved on, Chris and Ken were becoming strong Christians and walking in the power of the Holy Spirit. God had transformed them as a couple and a family and was now using them to minister to others. Also, a friendship had developed between us that has lasted 38 years.

Seven years after I met Chris and Denine, I gave birth to our second daughter, Megan. The doctors said she had multiple "congenital anomalies", a lot wrong at birth. Wrestling with terror in my heart of what was ahead of us, I thought about Chris lovingly stroking Denine's hair. We never know what life will bring our way but we do know that God is always there for us with His love, strength and help.

Looking back on the past 38 years, I am in awe of God's loving hand in our lives. He used Terry and me, a young inexperienced couple to introduce a family to His presence and power. That family, in turn, has shared His love with hundreds of hurting people. Together we all have learned that life is lived one step at a time embracing what comes and trusting God's ever present love to sustain and empower.

Karen Somerville, May 2016.

Chapter 1: Denine Kamillia

That night, something wasn't quite right. I wasn't able to sleep well. I kept waking up every hour or so. I wasn't in any pain, so what was this? My bed was wet! I thought I had given up bed-wetting years ago. But the bed was definitely wet. I got up and went to the bathroom, lugging my huge belly in front of me. Taking a towel to lay under me, I went back to bed, only to repeat the process over again several times through the night.

On my way back to bed after my fourth trip to the bathroom, I wet myself again and wondered what was going on. Then I realized that it wasn't urine I was leaking, but amniotic fluid, and it was happening every hour. I had been waiting to feel pain, and so I was unsure what to do.

I called my family doctor, who said, "Better not take any chances. Check into the hospital this morning." The date was Wednesday, July 25, 1973.

I waited for Ken to come in from the barn for breakfast, and around ten a.m. we drove to the hospital in Brantford. We waited—for what seemed like hours—to be properly admitted, and then I was escorted upstairs to an air-conditioned labour room to wait. Ken was not allowed to see me when any doctors or nurses were in the room, so he had a lonely wait outside. Lunch was brought in and Ken shared it with me (pea soup – yuk!).

This was my first baby, and I had taken prenatal classes for several months in preparation. But I wasn't really prepared for what was about to happen. There were still no pains, but the fluid kept seeping out at regular intervals. The nurses made all the necessary preparations, giving me an enema and shots, shaving me, and giving me a few extra shots for good measure.

Ken was in and out throughout that afternoon. Finally around six o'clock, I felt so sorry for him sitting there while nothing was happening that I suggested he go home. He did. I hoped that he would come back in the morning, but he didn't return until almost eight o'clock the next night.

I was all alone. This was my first night in a hospital and everyone around me was a complete stranger, except for my obstetrician, but he would not be back until the last moment, when he was needed. I was scared. I still wasn't feeling any pain, and I wondered if I'd made a mistake. No, I was already three days overdue, so this must be it. I had been waiting for my breasts to swell with milk, but no one told me that happens after the baby comes.

Around eight or nine in the evening I started feeling a fluttering in my lower back, every twenty minutes or so. When the feeling became stronger, I realized that I was in labour, finally. The fluttering soon turned to mild pains, and the time between them started to decrease: twenty minutes . . . ten minutes . . . five minutes. I called for a bedpan every hour, just as my prenatal instructor had told me to.

After eleven o'clock, everyone suddenly disappeared. There was no nurse checking on me every so often. It was so quiet, and then suddenly it wasn't; something was going on in the next room. The moans coming from the next room started out slow and intermittent, and became increasingly louder. Someone was in obvious distress. She carried on for several hours, hollering and screaming and cursing. It sounded like a torture chamber next door, and I was left scared and completely alone.

The pains were coming every two minutes now, and they were getting harder and harder to bear. They were all in my lower back and it was all I could do to watch the clock and breathe properly as I had been taught. I refused to cry out. I had too much self control—so I thought—to let go.

At two-thirty in the morning, I called a nurse for a bedpan. She finally arrived as I was relaxing from the worst pain yet. As I caught my breath, I commented on the severe pain I was in.

She got mad at me and said, "You can't call the nurse every time you have a pain. We're busy."

I was crushed. After all, I was there to have a baby. Meekly, I asked her again for a bedpan. She brought me an ice cold, stainless steel pan and left. She did not return. For twenty minutes I lay on top of that hard bedpan. The pains did not decrease in duration or intensity and I could not roll off the pan.

Again I called for a nurse and no one came. I wanted to throw up so badly. Finally, an elderly nurse came to remove the bedpan, and she brought me a tray to vomit into. I explained the intensity of the pain I was feeling, and she did a thorough investigation. She said I had not started to dilate yet, so I did not need any extra attention. She gave me a needle and left. For the next four hours, the pains slowed down to five-minute intervals and I managed to sleep for a few minutes between them.

At seven o'clock in the morning, the room suddenly burst into a hive of activity as the morning shift came in. I was given a breakfast tray, from which I only managed a couple swallows of apple juice. Next came a bed bath, followed by a new bedpan. I couldn't void if my life depended on it, so they inserted a catheter, which was agony. The pains started to increase in frequency and intensity again. What was that nurse doing? Everyone was doing so many different things and there was so much distraction that I got confused and was unable to concentrate on my breathing and watch the clock.

The first bearing down pain came. I panicked and started to hyperventilate. The pains were suddenly ten times worse!

A nurse at my side tried to calm me down, "You need to relax and get your breathing regulated. Breathe in for five seconds . . . good . . . now breathe out for five more. That's much better." I was able to relax for a moment.

But the nurse kept poking and prodding. It hurt. Throughout the next four hours, the bearing down pain came several more times, until they finally decided it was time to move me to the delivery room.

I couldn't understand where all these people had been at three a.m. when I had wanted someone so badly. The nurse at the prenatal classes had said that I wouldn't be left alone while I was in labour. But in the end, I was alone almost all night, in a strange hospital, having my first baby. And where was Ken? There was no phone to call him. He would be out of the house anyway, busy with work. After all, having babies was a common thing on the farm. His mother had five and each time his dad was at home working or sleeping. He would do the same.

I was on the delivery table. They covered my feet and legs with white leggings and put them up in stirrups. It felt awful. The pains were worse now, and I couldn't concentrate on breathing in that position. They brought out the catheter again. *Don't they know how much that thing hurts?* The doctor came in all garbed in green, and he suddenly had everything under control. It was another half hour before a dark haired, bright eyed, seven and a half pound baby girl was delivered, at 11:22 a.m. on Thursday, July 26, 1973. Four days earlier, I had turned twenty-one.

Ken arrived at the hospital at 7:45 that night. His first-born child was already nine hours old. Visiting hours were over at eight, so he only stayed fifteen minutes.

That was forty-three years ago. To this day, whenever I see a digital clock that says 11:22, I am reminded of Denine. On so many nights when I climb into bed our alarm clock registers 11:22. I don't want to forget her; I loved her too much to ever want to forget. Denine Kamillia: our first baby.

Chapter 2: My Family of Origin

I was born and raised on a dairy farm near Hamilton, Ontario, Canada. I was the fourth of seven children born to immigrant parents at the height of the baby boom generation. My parents met after World War II; he was a young Polish soldier, and she was a young Polish refugee.

At fifteen, Czeslaw decided that he didn't want to stay home and work on the tiny acreage that made up his family home in rural Poland. So, in 1935, he went off to school to become a butcher. He was the oldest of four. Two of his sisters died young and his other sister was only eight years old when he went away. He didn't see her again until he returned to Poland in 1966 to visit their mother, who died a few months later. After that, he never saw his sister again. At the beginning of World War II in 1939, he was among the thousands of young and old Polish males who were taken off to prison camps in Russia. He was also one of those who escaped. He spent the rest of the war cooking meals for troops in the British Armed Forces.

At thirteen, Halina's formal education ended when German troops marched into Warsaw and occupied the region. Her only brother died a few days later. She and her two sisters were among the insurgents who survived the 1944 Warsaw Rising: the sixty-three days that Polish citizens barricaded themselves in the Old City as a protest against occupying German troops. She was one of those who fully expected the Russian troops, camped a mere twelve kilometres east of the city, to come to their rescue. She was wrong. Her friends and neighbours were massacred and the few survivors were taken to an internment camp in Germany. Warsaw was totally destroyed by fire. After the devastation, the Russian troops moved in and drove out the Germans.

My parents met after the war when my father delivered food—the best Polish sausage ever I am told—to her refugee camp. They married and moved to Canada, where they raised seven children on a dairy farm. They often told stories of their wartime adventures to us young children, but as we got older, we became less interested.

We were an immigrant Catholic family living in a Protestant farming community. Because attending the local church was unthinkable, we attended church in the city once or twice a year. I was the middle of seven children. My older sisters were four and six years older than me. They shared a room. One brother was a year older and another a year younger. They shared a room. One winter, the five of us all slept in one bed together because there was no furnace. Since I was the only one who wet the bed, I was not very popular in that bed on those cold nights. This must have been the reason why I had a whole room to myself, later on. Until I married Ken, I wasn't used to sharing a room or a bed.

Two more siblings joined the crowd a few years later. A brother was born just before I started school at age six. We attended one of the last one-room schools in our county. Imagine the security of being in the same classroom as four of your siblings. All eight grades were taught by the same teacher. In my final year, there were twenty-four students. We mostly walked to and from school and home for lunch; we certainly did get lots of exercise! I enjoyed school and learning to read opened a whole new world to me. The one-room schools were all closed in 1962 and we were bused to a bigger school. Suddenly I found myself in a room filled with thirty other ten year olds. My sense of security fled and was replaced by a fear of bullying. That same year, my younger sister Amy was born, and I learned how babies come into existence. Amy once said that she didn't have three older sisters; she had four mothers.

Life on the farm was the only thing I knew. Everyone helped with the chores, but only the girls had to do house work. I grew up milking cows, driving tractors, and sneaking kittens into my bedroom. I was fourteen when we had an indoor bathroom installed in the corner of the back kitchen. Since it was not heated or insulated, the water pipes froze and cracked, so we had to take a pail of water from the kitchen to flush the toilet every single time. Still, it was definitely an improvement over the outhouse. My two older sisters both left home that year and I came to the realization that our father was an alcoholic.

Ken and I met through a local 4-H program. He belonged to clubs in the south of the county and I belonged to clubs in the north, and as the saying goes, never the twain shall meet. Our clubs were often friendly rivals in judging competitions and in showing our oats, corn, and calves at local fairs. We started dating the night before my eighteenth birthday. We went to a CFL football game (Saskatchewan in Hamilton), and after the game, we couldn't find where we had parked the car. Eventually we found it, and he kept me out until after midnight so he could give me a birthday present: a small box of chocolates. He got that one right.

My parents really liked him and so did my family. What wasn't to like about him? He was a polite, respectful, and hard-working young farmer. I had already been accepted into a home economics program at Kemptville College of Technology. It was my way of running away from home, but with the approval of my parents. Ken and I wrote to each other every day and mailed the letters once a week.

Ken made me feel like I was the most beautiful, most important person on the face of the earth. I wanted to spend the rest of my life with him. Actually, we wanted to have sex, but getting married first was the proper thing to do. So we got married. It was on a warm summer evening on the front lawn of his family farm that Ken and I vowed to love, honour, cherish, and be faithful to each other as long as we both lived. We were married for a year and a half before we learned that I was expecting. We were so excited as we prepared for the birth of our first child.

Chapter 3: Why is She So Stiff?

We brought Denine, our precious new daughter, home from the hospital when she was five days old. She had to stay an extra two days because her skin was showing signs of jaundice. I didn't mind. I was so worn out that I enjoyed the extra time to rest. All I had to do was sleep and feed her. The nurses did the rest. We took our baby home and laid her down between us on the bed. She was perfect. We marvelled at the waves in her dark brown hair, at the dimple on her chin that so resembled her daddy's, at her mother's eyebrows and those long fingers that might one day play the piano. We gazed into those big brown eyes, and we knew that she recognized us. What a joyful moment it was.

As time went on, we would discover that she always looked right at people with such big wide eyes. She was unable to blink.

Denine gained weight quickly in those first weeks. I was breast-feeding her, and she was a bit slow to get the knack of nursing, but then so was I. It was my first time too, and I had a lot to learn. I lost weight quickly until I was back down to 130 pounds, where I'd been a year earlier. I felt good, although my back did hurt at times. I was born with a curvature in my spine, and I had injured it four years earlier doing gymnastics in high school physical education.

At six weeks old, Denine ran a slight fever; it was nothing serious, but just enough to stop her from eating for one day. I was in agony as my milk supply was generous, and from that, I too ran a fever. We both felt better after a day or two. I discovered while nursing my baby that as she sucked a bit on the nipple, the milk would flow, and all she had to do was swallow. But she dribbled a lot. Since I was so new to all this, I took it in stride.

I had trouble bathing this tiny little human. It was something I'd never done before. As I would undress her, she would stiffen up. I thought she was cold, so I only bathed her once a week or so. According to the baby book, I didn't have the proper equipment. I didn't even have a draft free room. I made many mistakes, but I struggled on anyway.

One day I discovered a raw sore on her neck, likely from fabric rubbing against it. I wasn't sure if I was supposed to put powder on it to dry it out, or lotion to lubricate it. She developed a dandy case of cradle cap, but no one had told me how to treat it, so I did nothing. She did have lots of hair so

I was able to shampoo it. It was a learning process, and I did the best I could with the knowledge I had.

We made regular visits to our family doctor. He was young and just starting out. He too noticed her stiffening up a bit when he undressed her to examine her, but he didn't pay any attention to it. She had her shots regularly. The public health nurse came by soon after our Denine was born for a routine visit. She said she would come back four months later.

In the meantime, there were two other new babies at our church that summer. They had been born a month before ours. As I continued to sit in church every Sunday morning with my beautiful baby girl, I noticed something: she sat so quietly. The two baby boys were wriggling and squirming and kicking. *What a good baby I have, compared to those two,* I thought.

It was November when the public health nurse came by again. She was an elderly lady who had never married, and she seemed to really care about the people she went to see. We were sitting over tea when she remarked that Denine was not holding her head up by herself. At four months, she should be able to do that. She also hadn't started to laugh; oh she smiled, but she didn't laugh. The nurse played with her a bit and got her laughing hysterically, but her laughter was kind of strange.

"Why is she so stiff?" She wanted to know. These were questions I had been asking myself, but refused to ask out loud. And now they were being brought out in the open.

Denine at four months

I took her to my family doctor right away and asked the same questions. He had noticed the stiffness, but everything else seemed normal, so he hadn't paid much attention. We were sent to a pediatrician.

We went for our first specialist's appointment with our little girl. He was new to Canada, and it was hard to understand what he was saying, so we were confused. He ordered some blood tests, so we went to the hospital for her first series of blood tests. A day or two before Christmas, the specialist we had seen informed us that Denine's blood tests had shown a hypo thyroid problem. She was admitted to the hospital on Boxing Day.

By this time, I had her on a bottle and she was getting boiled skim milk from our dairy farm. She was even starting to eat solid food: a few peaches, applesauce, and rice cereal. Feedings were slow, but after all, I was just learning how to do it.

At the hospital, they ran some tests and started doing therapy. I questioned my family doctor about the tests and it turned out that the lab had made a mistake with the thyroid results. There was no thyroid problem, but they were alerted to the fact that there definitely was something wrong. A whole new series of tests was ordered.

We went back to the pediatrician. I became more confused. I started making weekly trips into Brantford for therapy sessions. The therapist did all these exercises with Denine while I sat and watched. It was so hot in there that I would doze off and not pay much attention to what was going on. I had no idea how serious it all was. I did some exercises at home with her, but they seemed useless to me.

Nov 30, 1973

Medical observations: four months old
  -keeps her head back all the time
  -when looking she has to extend her neck much more which is common with dropping eyelids or defective vision
  -on 2% milk, gaining weight poorly only 4 oz in past few weeks
  -not roll over – which is rather doubtful
  -does follow objects
  -her hearing is questionable
  -examination shows a normally developed infant physically, with normal height and weight for age
  -signs are suggestive of mental retardation
  -she has spastic quadriplegia which probably results from cerebral palsy
  -short neck and puffy cheeks
  -head size 15.2" is small for the size of her body
  -droopy eyelids
  -eyes are always bright open
  -hearing seems to be absent
  -stiffness of the neck and all the joints
  -anterior fontanel small
  -seems to have neurological disorder
  -suggest some degree of retardation

Conclusion: I think this infant has cerebral palsy, spastic quadriplegia and possible mental retardation. Ordered skull x-ray, neck, skeletal survey, T3T4, epiphysis to rule out hypothyroid and chromosome analysis. Have not declared retardation to the mother but have given some hint that there may be some slowness involved and will have to investigate further before final diagnosis be established.

Results: MUMC Regional Cytogenetic Lab

-brought her to the lab on February 8, 1974

-peripheral blood sample obtained from cell

-second analysis of D. Chromosomes

-carried out with fluorescent banding

-father -unusually shaped No. 22 chromosome

-Denine: normal female karyotype

Chapter 4: More Tests

One day in March, the pediatrician informed us that there seemed to be some brain damage. He'd try to make an appointment for us with a specialist in Toronto. He told us that if we didn't hear anything within a month, to call his office. The next day, I saw our family doctor and repeated all this. He said that if there was any chance of brain damage, we should not waste any time. Two days later, Ken and I found ourselves in the waiting room of a high rise medical clinic in downtown Toronto. This doctor was middle aged and seemed nice enough. We went through the usual preliminaries involved with seeing a new doctor, and finally he examined Denine. He measured her head several times, and when I asked why, the doctor explained that according to the development graphs, her head should be a certain size at a certain age. If it was not, there was a problem. It could be that her brain was not growing as quickly as it ought to be.

She was now eight months old, and up until this time, she had been gaining weight progressively. We discussed the possibility of admitting her to a Toronto hospital for extensive testing. Since we lived a long hour's drive away, we asked if she could be admitted that same day. He said that he would see what he could do.

We found our way to the hospital and went through the usual channels of admittance (Why do they always take so long?). They gave her a hospital gown and sent us to a waiting area. Six hours later, we were informed that they had a bed ready. We were escorted to the allocated room to begin the second phase of admittance.

They asked us many questions that first day: What specific problems have you noticed? What does she eat? Does she sleep on her stomach or back? What does she not like? When did she laugh first? The questioning went on and on. Finally, she was settled in for—what we thought would be—three days of extensive testing. We were wrong. She got pneumonia while she was there. She also cut her first four teeth in that hospital.

After three weeks, the doctor informed us that they were going to do an operation. They felt it was necessary to insert a shunt from her brain to her stomach. I understood that this meant they would insert a small tube to drain the cystic fluid that was putting pressure on her brain. The date and time were set. We waited at home . . . and waited and waited.

The doctor was supposed to call after the operation. He did not. After waiting all afternoon by the phone, I called him at the hospital. After a long wait on a long distance line, he finally came on and said that they hadn't done the operation that morning. They had shaved the top of her head, drained off some fluid, and filled it with air, only to discover that there was no pressure being put on the brain. So, they did not do the operation. We were told that we could pick her up the next day and given a time to meet him at the hospital. Were we so unimportant that he could not call to tell us what had happened? Or was he just too busy?

The next day, we arrived at the hospital at the appointed hour and had to wait for him. After a while, we were ushered into a small classroom with a blackboard. The doctor proceeded to quietly and simply explain the type of brain damage Denine had, how severe it was, and what he would recommend that we do.

It appeared that very early in my pregnancy, about eight weeks in, the fetus had suffered a stroke of some sort, which had blocked blood vessels to the brain. As the organs were still developing at the time, there was a reduced blood supply to the brain, which was just beginning to form. He drew a diagram of the brain on the board and started to cut out pieces here and there to show which parts of Denine's brain had not formed. By the time he was finished, nearly half the brain had been removed. These vacant parts were filled with fluid. Initially, they had thought there was pressure, but it turned out that there wasn't. This was such a rare thing that there was no documented record of it having happened before. Her condition was so severe that there was no hope of her getting better.

His recommendations were rather drastic. He said, "If I could have my way, I'd take this child away and never let you take her home."

I think he wanted to spare us what he knew was ahead. He was wrong. I had a friend who took that very same advice, and she shared her story with me. She let the experts arrange to put her five month old baby girl in an institution, and she never saw her again. Her child died two years later. Now after thirty years, her heart is still very sore. The recommendation was supposed to help her with her two boys at home, but she says that to this day, she is unable to sing "Away in a Manger" without breaking into tears of regret. As a minister's wife, she has often broken into such tears.

We gathered Denine and her things and prepared to leave the hospital. Before we could leave, we had to pick up a prescription at the pharmacy downstairs. Fortunately, we had enough money on us. It was not cheap.

March 21, 1974

Medical Observations: eight months old

    -retardation and chromosomal error

    -slow milestones

    -does not roll over yet

    -makes noises all the time

    -smiles at everybody

    -is more or less meaningless

    -immunized for DPTP

    -height: 27", weight: 16 ½ lbs (both in fifty percent: excellent growth)

    -has long hair

    -thrusts her tongue like a snake (can happen sometimes with frontal lobe lesions)

    -dermoid cyst over the philtrum

    -anterior fontanel is closed

    -head size is 16.4" (small in relation to the rest of the physical development)

    -no teeth yet

    -slight cleft palate

    -upturned nose

    -hands show flexion contracture which occurs with tri somi 17-18

    -spasticity of extremities is still present (suggest seven drops of Valium four times per day, reduced later)

    -chokes when being fed and drinking, usually associated with mio-ordination of the deglutition

    -keeps her head back all the time, and when looking up she has to extend her neck much more, which is common with drooping eyelids or defective vision

Chapter 5: Home Again

At twenty-one years of age, I was not well-informed on some things. Oh, I had gone through the average Canadian high school program and studied languages, sciences, and math. I had learned that I was not much of an athlete, and that I preferred to sit and read. I majored in home economics at a small agricultural college. I had learned to make terrific pies, how to set a table, how to read a dress pattern, and how to sew some beautiful things. But I had not learned anything about institutions for the severely disabled.

My only knowledge of such places came from television, which had portrayed these institutions as cold, white sterile cells where they throw someone in, lock the door, and throw away the keys. An avid reader of old historical novels, I was reminded of old "insane asylums", dungeons of torture from which you could never return once you were locked up. No, I had no idea what the doctor was talking about when he wanted to commit my baby to a government institution. But I had some awful preconceived notions at the time.

How could I let them lock away my little girl forever? I thought I would never see her again if I let this happen. She would be just a vegetable among other vegetables. What would happen if she died? Would we be able to bring her home and bury her in the family plot? These thoughts and others far worse, passed through my mind as I carried my precious little bundle of baby girl home. And I cried.

During the three weeks that Denine was in the Toronto hospital, we told no one except Ken's parents. They in turn told no one; they were always rather private with family problems. It was Ken's request that we keep it to ourselves; I don't think he was able to face what was going on. It was too much to talk about such a dreadful possibility. So we kept it to ourselves. He was able to throw himself into his farming; seeding time was here and there was plenty to do.

It was different for me. While Denine was away in the hospital, the house was so empty. I had no baby to feed, no baby to change, no baby crying, no baby to cuddle, and no baby to wake me in the middle of the night. During that time, I took on a challenging sewing project and completed it. My back, which usually bothered me off and on, seemed to hurt almost all the time now. I would soon find out that the more stress I was facing, the more my back would hurt.

When Denine arrived home, she was quite a sight. She had four lovely new teeth. But the top part of her beautiful dark wavy hair had been shaved off. It was bristly and stubbly and it felt strange to touch her head. I put little caps and bonnets on her to hide the shaved area and left the back part long. As the top grew, I trimmed the back to even it up.

Usually when babies reach the teething stage, they put their fists into their mouths and chew on them. Denine was no different. As she relaxed, she would let her head drop forward, and somehow, she managed to get her hand into her mouth. The only problem was, with four new teeth, she bit herself. She would clamp down on her finger and panic, thereby biting herself harder and harder. She would be unable to let go until she came up for a breath of air to cry. Her fingers would fall out of her mouth, and that would be that. She bit herself a lot. We brought it to the doctor's attention, but there was nothing that could be done.

Those first four days after we brought her home were very trying. We were just getting used to the fact that our baby was "severely retarded." There was no hope, no hope, and again, no hope. And we believed them. I mean, how could she grow half a brain that just wasn't there? I cried every time I looked at her. I cried when I fed her. I cried when I changed her. A friend phoned me asking about her and I tried to explain what the doctor had said, but I just cried.

We asked our minister to come and see us. We needed to talk this over with someone. We discussed what we had seen and what the doctors had said. He shared with us how he had a brother who, at the age of ten, had been placed in an institution. And I suddenly realized that we were not the only ones. There were others who had gone through what we were going through. That afternoon, I made a firm decision. We would place her in a home someday, but not until we knew that the time was right.

I did not cry again. I went on to face the world with my handicapped girl. Those weeks following her arrival back home were filled with appointments and doctors. We saw the family doctor and had a long talk with him. He was all for helping us with finding a placement in an institution. He offered to use his authority and influence as a doctor to help us. His own brother had been forced to place his baby in an institution, and it had taken a long time, but he would help if we wanted him to.

We went to the Children's Aid Society to seek help. The information we received there was very interesting and helped with my peace of mind. They said, "We could find a foster home for Denine, but really, that would only allow for an older, more experienced woman to look after her. She might as well stay with you. You obviously love her so much." So, we closed that door and never looked back.

We were put in touch with a pediatrician from Chedoke Family Practice Unit who specialized in handicapped children. We attended our first assessment clinic. I forget who was present, but I remember that there was Denine, Ken and myself, the public health nurse, the pediatrician, a physiotherapist, a speech therapist, a lady who did counselling, and a couple of others. We spent two and a half hours going over the entire history of my pregnancy, my delivery, and anything else they could think of. We'd gone through all this already with all the other doctors, but we went through the list again, for the fourth time in as many months.

No, I did not drink alcohol. No, I was not on any drugs. No, I did not smoke. No, I had not had any major mishaps. I started weekly iron shots one month before I conceived. I got a routine series of vaccinations at the same time. My nausea lasted three months. I felt the first movement at sixteen weeks: just light flutters. No, not too active. She pressed mostly in one spot. I gained almost thirty pounds. No vomiting. I carried her high. I experience lots of indigestion. I had leg cramps the last few weeks. Even through the whole labour and delivery process, everything had been as normal as could be expected. No, nothing happened during delivery to cause her problems. There was no history of anything like this in either family. I answered all these questions, and more.

After asking all their questions, they undressed Denine and started examining her very thoroughly. They poked, prodded, twisted, turned, listened, and looked until the poor child was quite distressed. Finally, they all left the room for a while and I was able to dress my precious child and hold her and cuddle her back into a good mood.

While the doctors discussed their examination findings, the public health nurse and the counsellor came back and started asking even more questions – very personal ones this time. Ken, being a very reserved and private person—he would not even hold hands in public back then—was quite upset by the whole thing. But I'm the one who finally broke down and lost my temper. I said some unkind things about my husband, and the counsellor decided we had marriage problems. She arranged for the two of us to attend a session to discuss the intimate details of our relationship.

We saw her once. She tried to draw out the most private details of our married life, and this made Ken really embarrassed. On the way home he announced, "There's nothing wrong with our relationship! We don't have any problems!" He refused to go back, and I didn't blame him. He didn't even talk to me about the things this woman was asking about.

Our relationship at this time seemed pretty normal. We had been married nearly three years. We were twenty-two years old and we were both healthy, well adjusted people. Neither of us ever drank, smoked, or did drugs. Ken is a quiet man, who listens far more than he speaks. I'm the opposite; I speak before I think and I often say things I regret later. Ken was so upset by these clinics and assessments that he stopped going. After all, he had a farm to work and it was getting into haying season. He was just too busy. I'd have to go by myself. And I did for the next four years. I'd come home each time and tell him everything that I could remember. He only ever heard my side of things.

What I didn't realize in those days was how much my husband was hurting inside. He kept that to himself because he was unable to verbalize it at the time. Years later, he told me that one day while he was lying on the couch holding Denine, he lifted her high above his head and told God that he would never get this close to anyone again because it hurt too much. As a result, he spent less and less time with his daughter. When he did come in from the barn or the field, he ate and laid down for a nap. He played ball with his younger brothers or his friends. I was not included.

April 2, 1974

Neurosurgical standpoint
-Cornelia de Lange Syndrome
- neurosurgical standpoint – obvious microcephaly is in part responsible for her spasticity and lack of development milestones
-suggest EEG skull films and brain scan – def. info. on long term outlook

Chapter 6: Cerebral Palsy Centre

We started taking Denine to the Cerebral Palsy Centre at Chedoke Hospital in Hamilton, a fifteen-minute drive from our farm. For the next two years, I would drive in with Denine every week to meet with one of the two therapists that had been assigned to work with us.

As I sat and waited each week for our session, I was fascinated by the activity that went on around me. A group of five or six children would make their way down the hall from one classroom to another. For these children with cerebral palsy, this was a school. It was set up in classroom format, complete with a small gymnasium, play area, and even a pool outside. Each child used whatever means was best suited for him or her to go from here to there. One would have braces and use crutches to walk. Another would lay on a board with wheels and push himself with his hands. Still another would use a walker. Some would be pushed in wheelchairs. The teachers called loud, simple encouragements to each child and they responded by getting there as best they could.

As I watched these children, I thought how wonderful it was that they were able to get around this much on their own. But Denine was different. There was no hope of her getting any better. At the time, I could only focus on what we were going to work on each day. After all, my girl didn't have Cerebral Palsy like these other children. How little I knew.

The speech therapist tried different ways of stimulating Denine to eat better. Her sucking ability was weak and her mouth was unable to form a vacuum to suck more efficiently, which resulted in liquids running out from the corners of her mouth. A specially shaped soother was prescribed and we would have to either hold it to her mouth with our hand or find some other way to fasten it. I found that transparent tape held the soother on, and if I was careful not to leave it on for too long, it did not irritate the skin of her cheeks too much. When I ran out of transparent tape, I used anything I could find, usually masking tape or sometimes, black hockey tape. There was always some of that around in case of emergency.

When Denine was first born, I had offered her a soother to help quiet her mood, but my mother-in-law disapproved greatly of those "dirty things" and she made me feel quite inadequate as a mother. Besides, Denine never wanted to keep the thing in anyway. At the time, I didn't realize why. When we gave it to her later on, when we started attending the Cerebral Palsy Centre, she attacked it. She sucked away a mile a minute, and she was constantly wet with drool. After a couple of years, she found a way to push the soother out with her tongue and get rid of it altogether. She no longer needed that kind of stimulation. But while she would bear it, we gave it to her as often as we felt necessary, which was often.

The speech therapist worked out different ways of holding Denine in order to feed her. Up until this time, I was feeding her in two different positions. For bottle-feeding, I held her in the usual way, in my left arm with my elbow propped up on a cushion or armrest. I put a pillow behind my back for support and sat in an old maple rocking chair. I made the hole in the nipple quite large, and milk often dribbled down her chin, through my arm, and onto the woodwork. We saturated many a washcloth in the process. The feedings often took up to an hour, in which time she could get through one eight-ounce bottle. As she worked with her soother and developed stronger suction capabilities, feeding times became more manageable.

To feed her solids up, I had until that point, propped her in an antique high chair with a small seat so she fit easily, a cushion or towel behind her back, a belt around her tummy, and as she started falling over, a hand behind her head. Not knowing at the time that she had any specific problems, I had just tried to feed her normally with a small spoonful of various baby foods. I would shovel the food in and she would push it back out. This went on and on and I would have to be quick to catch it and return it to her mouth. She was trying to eat, but her natural reflexes were not developed and she just kept pushing the food back out with her tongue.

We tried to encourage chewing in lots of different ways. We rubbed her gums with a finger to get her jaw going up and down. We fed her pieces of chocolate chip cookies and rubbed her gums with each piece. As her sucking power increased, she was able to chew things a little bit better. But as she started to develop teeth, a new problem developed; she would clamp down on a finger and she wouldn't let go. She would then panic and bite harder and harder, until she finally let go. There was no way to pull your finger out once it was trapped. This became a game of either quick reflexes or patience. My patience often ran out quickly and she did not get as much chewing stimulation as she might have. Denine would bite herself if she found a way to get her finger in her mouth. Often, she bit down until she drew blood.

We tried getting her to drink from a cup. This was tricky and very messy and we spilled more than she drank. We bought a special cup for her that was shaped so that the liquid could be poured in sideways without spilling out everywhere. But even with this special cup, if she got her teeth closed on it, she panicked.

The physiotherapist tried many different things to stimulate Denine. She rolled her on tubes and balls. She sat with her on the floor and exercised her arms and legs. When we started, they measured her and determined exactly how far they were able to stretch, bend, twist, or straighten each of her arms and legs, her head, and each of her fingers. Then they worked with each limb to try to get it to bend, stretch, or straighten even further.

She kept her fists clenched most of the time and sometimes her fingers would relax a bit. She was laid on her stomach and her legs were bent this way and that and her arms were turned and raised and lowered. They tried to get her to roll over. They tempted her with bright toys that rewarded her with noise and movement at the slightest touch. Many of these exercises caused her to cry or whine in complaint. When this carried on for too long, Denine was handed to me for a few minutes of cuddling. When I held her, she stopped fussing and was happy.

Since the exercises caused her so much distress, I did not persist with them at home. I went through the motions each day, but never for too long. I could not see any real progress anyway, and we had been told there was no hope, so why bother? We still had regular assessment clinics with our team of professionals, but I went alone now.

Chapter 7: Coping

For her first birthday, my father bought Denine an infant car seat. In 1974 there were no laws concerning safety seats for babies and these car seats were new. This quickly became the piece of furniture we used most often with Denine for the next year. Weighing approximately sixteen pounds, Denine was flexible enough to sit cross-legged in this seat. There was a belt on it to secure her and she fit beautifully and comfortably. This seat made it much easier to feed her because her head was held back at a convenient angle; it was angled back just far enough for the food not to fall out, and yet not too far back for her to choke on it.

I found it so much easier to do my grocery shopping with this seat. Before, I had always tried to sit her in the front part of the shopping cart, provided for children. When she was in a snowsuit she fit comfortably, but she kept falling to one side or the other and she couldn't stop herself from falling.

When she fell over too often for me to keep straightening her, I let her stay lying over sideways and propped my large purse under her head for support. We got many strange looks, but I chose to ignore them for the most part. I was more than willing to speak about my baby, if someone stopped to ask me about her. I was very proud of her, in spite of all the problems she was encountering. Once we got the car seat, I was able to set it inside the shopping cart and pile the groceries all around her. It made things so much easier.

Denine's new car seat

For the first two years of our marriage, Ken used to take me grocery shopping. Once Denine was old enough to come to the store, I went alone with her. As time went on, Ken was less willing to be seen with her in public. He could choose to stay home and not face the world with this child who was different, but I could not. I was forced to take her out among other people: to the doctor's office, to therapy, grocery shopping, to visit friends and family, and even to church. We were unable to afford a baby sitter back then, and I wasn't willing to leave my baby behind anyway.

In the fall, Ken joined a hockey team with a number of guys he had gone to school with. This was a non-contact industrial hockey league. There were six teams from the Hamilton area that played on Sunday evenings. Since Ken was unwilling to have his daughter out in public around "his" friends, I was forced to leave her at home if I wanted to go watch him play. I managed to talk his mother into babysitting most Sunday nights. Attending Ken's hockey games was a chance to get away from home and from the problems that were developing there, so I was eager to go. This being said, hockey did not excite me; wasting all that energy chasing a tiny puck around seemed stupid to me. But being around people did excite me and that's what I needed at that time. I still knew very few people in the neighbourhood and there were other young mothers, and the girlfriends of some players, that I could spend time with and feel normal for two hours a week.

We often got together for team parties on Friday or Saturday nights. The fact that we didn't drink didn't stop us from enjoying the company of the other young adults. Ken was the only one that had to get up and go to work in the mornings; cows had to be milked on Sunday mornings too. As we drove home from these parties, he would criticize me for all the things he had heard me tell the people there. I thought, *we'll see if I ever talk to him again*. I would keep my feelings from him and avoid speaking to him for a few days after.

Our relationship with Ken's parents was rather interesting at that time. Ken worked on the farm with his father. This had been the arrangement since he was eighteen and he finished high school. He lived at home with his parents and had room and board deducted from his wages. When he planned on marrying a year later, his parents built a lovely new house for themselves across the yard from the twelve-room, 1840's brick farmhouse that they had always lived in. They were vacating the house so that we could have a home together, as husband and wife. We were married in the summer and the new house was not completed until mid-December. So, in the early days of my marriage, I moved in with my new husband and his family: his father and mother, his fourteen-year-old sister, his four and five-year-old brothers, and a hired man.

Now, Ken's parents were two of the most beautiful, unselfish people I knew. They often made allowances for the plans of their children. Many times they changed their plans to accommodate ours. Living under the same roof for those months was tolerable because we knew they would be moving out soon, and then we could start our married life together, alone.

In the meantime, Ken's mother ruled the house. It was her house, and she did the planning and the shopping and the cooking. She was the boss. I helped out as much as I could, but I seldom offered to do anything unless I was asked. I was not accustomed to living in a house that was run as neatly and efficiently as this one was. So I watched and learned and tried to stay out of trouble. I spent as much time with my husband as I could. The only place we could be alone was in our bedroom, but we couldn't spend all day there. There was work to be done. After we got married, the only thing that changed for Ken was that now he had a wife in his bed when he came home from work. I had to change my whole lifestyle and learn to live with a new family that were set in their ways. When his parents did finally move into their new home, we were able to start our married life together, alone at last.

As time went on, I realized that although I had been forced to adapt to the Forster lifestyle, Ken had not had to change his lifestyle until after his parents and family moved out. When it was finally just the two of us living in the house, he expected everything to be run the same way it always had been. I was expected to use his mother's recipes and cook the same things she did, to manage the finances as she did, and so much more. We rented the house from them, but they left many things behind when they moved out. Several rooms remained filled with stuff that had collected over the decades: old furniture, magazines, books, and picture frames.

It became bondage to me. I could not buy new furniture because there was already furniture there, but it wasn't mine and I felt guilty using it. When I finally did put some of it to use, one of his family members would come and lay claim to it and take it from the house. I struggled with what to do in that situation. They didn't want the stuff, but we could not get rid of it. So, some was used and some was stored in a couple of unused rooms and ignored. Over time, we did collect our own things, and eventually our twelve-room house became very, very cluttered.

They left us their old freezer, dryer, wringer, washer, and stove. They even bought us a new refrigerator. Looking back, I see now that we were so blessed with all of these appliances, but I never saw it that way. To me, everything was old. It was all unwanted stuff, second hand . . . rejected. I did not dare paint or paper anything; after all, it was not my house.

We also rented the farm pickup truck. We had an arrangement that the pickup truck was available for us to use when the farm did not need it. That first year we were married, we drove to church, to the grocery store, and to my parents. The second year I added a few trips to the doctor and to prenatal classes. The third year, extra visits to the doctor and to therapy were added for Denine, and now weekly hockey games joined the list. Ken heard so many comments from his family about the amount of driving we were doing and the price of gas that eventually I felt weighed down by even more guilt.

On top of all this, I was now forced to ask my mother-in-law to babysit her only grandchild. She was not thrilled. After all, she had three children of her own, a husband and a hired man to look after, but she always took Denine when I asked her and many times she changed her own plans to help me. I did not appreciate her sacrifices; I was only thinking about my own selfish wants. At the time, Denine would cry most of the time I was away. I would always assure Grandma that she was fed and ready for bed, and I would give her an extra bottle just in case, but still Denine cried so often in my absence that they found it a burden. But at the same time, I needed to get out. So I went.

After that initial assessment clinic, life took on a whole different meaning. The ball had started rolling and we were introduced to the world of handicapped and crippled children. In my twenty-two years of life before that time, I could only remember encountering one handicapped child. She was the daughter of a friend of my parents. The mother had German measles during her pregnancy. I could recall this girl, Sophie, who was a year older than me, sitting on the floor chewing a skipping rope and drooling, oh she drooled so much. She could only walk if someone held her hands to balance her. I was twelve when I last saw her, and my last impression of her was that of a baby in a teenager's body. If this was what I had to look forward to in ten to twelve years, then I wanted to be prepared.

Ken and I had both always wanted to have several children, so we discussed the possibility of having a second baby while

Denine was still young. I felt it would make things harder as Denine grew if we waited. We sought our doctor's advice. German measles were passing through our neighbourhood that summer so he suggested that we wait until I was tested to be sure I'd had the measles as a child.

When we discovered that we were going to have a second baby, we were overjoyed. We told no one. Ken did not want anyone to know until I was too big to hide it. He had done the same with Denine. I grew in size and my back started hurting more than usual (I had the added weight of Denine to carry around now). She still had her weekly therapy sessions and she screamed as much as ever, but a truck ride always made her doze. I was as happy as I could be under the circumstances.

A friend of mine was pregnant at the same time and she was greatly concerned about my having a second handicapped baby. She said that she would be so afraid and would have tests done to see if the baby was okay or not. But I refused, because it didn't matter. If the tests were not normal, would I abort my baby? Never. Who was I to take a life that God had created in me? To murder a human being because it was not perfectly formed, it was inconceivable. I would rather not know beforehand and accept another handicapped baby than to even consider any alternatives. At this time, I was forced to take a good look at the possibility of abortion, and I wiped it out completely. I knew that I would never be able to take that step. To me, it was murder. Period. Besides, I had confidence that I would bear a healthy son; we never even considered any girls names.

Chapter 8: High Fever

The happiness I was feeling did not last long. A few months later Ken got a dreadful case of tonsillitis and was home sick for a couple of days. As he waited in the doctor's office, I carried Denine over my protruding tummy in a bitterly cold wind to a nearby store to buy a chocolate bar. I never thought how cold it was for her. The next day she started to run a fever. As she got hotter, I bundled her up cozy and warm in a baby quilt and cuddled her. I made a doctor's appointment for the afternoon. One thing about our family doctor was that we always had confidence that if any of us were sick, he would see us that same day, not the next week when they could work us in.

As the hour approached, I took Denine's temperature and it was 105.5 F. I called his office and asked if he would come to the house to see her, but he would not. He said to bundle her up lightly and bring her in right away. I was scared.

She had picked up the flu and was very sick. She was admitted to the hospital in Brantford right away. We went through the usual routine of filling out charts and forms. This time she had her car seat and soother, but they quickly lost her soother. I also took a carton of yogurt and wheat germ, which she liked to eat.

I came home from the hospital several hours later to my sick husband and told him everything that had happened.

He said, "Maybe she'll even die."

She can't die! I thought. *She's my baby! How dare he say such a thing! Doesn't he care about her at all?* I knew that he was being realistic.

At bedtime, I went into her empty room. I looked at her crib and her toys and clothes and I prayed, "God, please don't take her from me. I couldn't bear to lose her." I did not release the pent up tears. Two days later, she came home perfectly healthy but she was a bit weaker.

I was suddenly faced with a problem. Ken and I were going away for the weekend to the King Edward Hotel in Toronto for a 4H leader's conference. This would be his first weekend off in nearly four years. It was so important for us to go, for us to get away together. It would cost us almost nothing because the county 4H clubs were sponsoring him and another leader. It was our big chance, but I had no babysitter! My mother was too busy milking cows to take Denine. My two brothers had suddenly left home. My father was sick. Ken's mother was sick. I tried asking friends of ours, but no one could look after her. Early Friday morning, I phoned my mother's neighbour Jane, and she was glad to take Denine. Half an hour later, I left Denine and her food and diaper bag with Jane, her husband, and their six kids and went to Toronto for two days. It was a wonderful weekend.

I picked up Denine on Sunday afternoon to find out that she hadn't eaten a thing for two days. It wasn't surprising; they didn't know how to feed her. It was only the third time they'd seen her, and they weren't used to the specialized job. Denine came home weak, but hungry, so I fed her. But within a few days she was running another fever, with a temperature of 104.5 F. What was I supposed to do now? I remembered that I shouldn't bundle her up, that I should keep her cool and have her drink plain water. Despite my best efforts, she wouldn't drink anything. She kept on crying and whining and she wouldn't go to sleep. I was getting so tired but I couldn't go to sleep. The next day, the fever still had not gone down, so I took her to the doctor. He prescribed some antibiotics and baby's aspirin and sent us home.

That night we didn't sleep again. I was too tired to stay up with her, so I lay down on the couch with her and held her. She was quieter when I held her. The fever was still high. All of the sudden, she started throwing herself backwards and jerking all over. She seemed stiffer and she was clenching her teeth. After what seemed like an hour, she finally settled down and we both dozed off. As I heard Ken leave the house at five a.m., I gathered up my sleeping girl, laid her in her crib, and went to bed myself. She slept most of the day.

When I saw the pediatrician again I told him what had happened, and he had so many questions. He wanted to know if it was a seizure or a convulsion. I didn't know, so I described it as best I could. We called it a "spell" for lack of a better word. He put her on liquid Valium and ordered a tepid bath to bring her fever down. Three weeks later, she ran another fever. I started her on the aspirin and again took her to the doctor. He gave her more antibiotics and sent us home again. Our middle of the night routine was repeated. This pattern repeated itself several times in the next four to five months.

I was getting much larger and sleeping was not easy for me. In May of that year, the doctor had Denine admitted as a day patient to McMaster Medical Centre for some new tests. I sat with her all day waiting for her to void for a urine sample, and it wasn't until I slipped downstairs to the cafeteria that she finally did. Even after these tests, they were not able to determine anything.

A couple of weeks later, she went through another three nights of spells. I called my doctor early one morning and told him what was happening. Later in the morning I called the pediatrician and he had us go back to McMaster for more tests. This time she was still running a high fever, but they still found nothing. Then all of a sudden, the fevers stopped. After five months of high fevers, sleepless nights, and spells, everything stopped. The doctors never did discover what they were and why everything stopped.

Denine's therapy sessions were greatly interrupted during those five months. I did not do her exercises with her very often or very well for that matter. Five months earlier, she could sit alone for a time, and now she could not be bent into a sitting position at all.

She was outgrowing her car seat. She was starting to push and strain her limbs. She would often get one leg pushed out of the seat and twist her body around until she almost fell out. Something had to be done, so we bought a larger child car seat. It was bigger and she fit it quite well, but it didn't really suit her needs. It had been getting harder and harder to carry her around over my pregnant belly. As I was shopping one day, I spotted a display of strollers. I sat Denine in every single one until I found one that gave in the right place and still supported her adequately. I wheeled her up to the cash register, paid for the stroller, and never looked back. What freedom!

Chapter 9: Daniel Kenneth

The spring and summer of 1975 was busy. My brothers no longer wanted to work on the farm and they had all left home, so our parents had no choice but to sell the farm. They moved into town and began receiving a veteran's pension. Ken played summer hockey. We were invited to six weddings and several showers. I needed a new dress, so I made a light yellow print dress big enough for me and for my tummy. Ken's younger sister was one of the brides and I was due two days before her wedding. I had visions of showing up at the maternity ward with confetti in my hair.

One of the weddings we attended was a gala Jewish event for Ken's friend, who had been his best man at our wedding. Three hundred and fifty people attended, and between courses I could only sit and watch. I had nowhere in my belly to put food. It was truly a sight to behold.

When all was said and done, I went into labour a full ten days ahead of schedule. I had spent the morning weeding my garden and then took a refreshing shower before lunch. As I lay down for a nap after lunch, my water broke and I soaked the bed. But I was elated; my baby was coming early! My parents immediately came over to pick up Denine and take her for a few days, and I waited for Ken to come home.

Ken was annoyed that I wanted to go to the hospital right away. He figured we'd have to wait for days, and as a result, he drove to town very slowly. I sat on a towel; I wasn't taking any chances this time. As we walked into the main entrance of the hospital, my water gushed out in full force and made quite a mess. I was quickly escorted up to the labour room and a cleaning lady mopped up the long corridor. Ken wanted to crawl under a rock.

He was left to do the admitting and I got all ready to have a baby. My labour pains started after breakfast the next morning. Needless to say, Ken was already back home working. This time, my labour took a different form; the pains were in my front and in my legs. My back was comfortable for a change. Seven hours later, I gave birth to a bouncing bundle of baby boy. He was so eager to start living, he cried before he was even out. Our son Daniel was born at 4:10 p.m. on Tuesday, July 8, 1975. My recovery was quick, but Daniel was jaundiced and remained in hospital for five days, just as his sister had before him.

I nursed Daniel and suddenly discovered what it was like to have a normal hungry baby. When he was brought for feedings, he attacked. He wriggled and squirmed, and I nearly lost him a few times. He kicked so much that the towel would not stay wound around him. He had healthy lungs and he knew how to use them. He also had a temper.

Ken was so proud of his new son. We took him home from the hospital Sunday afternoon and on the way home we stopped in at his mother's to show off her first grandson. He got to meet his aunts and uncles at the trousseau tea at her house that afternoon. The wedding was the following Saturday and I wore a different new dress. This one was not quite so full.

Denine came home from my mother's and my younger sister Amy came to stay with us for a while. At thirteen, she was more than capable of helping me with the new baby and with caring for Denine. But more importantly, she was another person for me to talk to. Beside her new baby brother, Denine was suddenly a great big girl. She enjoyed having him around, but pretty soon I noticed that every time I fed him, she cried to be fed. It was awkward to feed them both at the same time. Though Denine was older, I still had two babies.

At five days old, on the day he came home from the hospital, Daniel also got to see his daddy play hockey. I now had a baby I could show off to the other hockey wives. I had only taken Denine to the arena once, because I had no sitter, and Ken was very annoyed. He could not bear to see his handicapped child there in public before his friends, and he would not allow me to take her again. And yet, I was only looking for attention and approval at the time. The people who came to speak to me and Denine were truly concerned and interested. They did not make me feel ashamed of her. And I was never ashamed of her. After all, she was a part of me and I loved her so much. As a result of these experiences, I started pouring more and more love into my children, and less and less into my relationship with my husband.

Denine and Daniel

Daniel progressed so quickly, while Denine did not develop very much at all. We started going to more hockey parties and games and I was now able to get Amy to come out to babysit on weekends. We bought a new sofa bed that summer and I finally had a place where I could sit and really relax and feel comfortable.

That summer, Denine had a new chair designed especially to suit her specific needs. It was a remarkable piece of artwork in my mind; it had a padded chair with a footrest and a seat belt. Since she had outgrown her infant car seat, we needed something else to sit her in during feedings. I still held her in my arms for bottle feedings. I always would.

Chapter 10: Dirty Dishes & Diapers

As I write this, I am sitting atop a high hill overlooking a beautiful and peaceful countryside. It is springtime and the sun is shining. A gentle breeze is blowing and the birds are singing. Big fluffy clouds are floating by with a gentle hint of rain to come. There is a quietness in my heart that says it's good to be alive. Life is so full of good things. God is in heaven and all is right with the world. I have learned to see the good in things, the good in people, and the good that can come with many situations.

It wasn't always so. Those months following Daniel's birth were hard months for me. They were hard to live through, and now looking back, they are hard to write about and relive. There was a restlessness in my soul; I felt that I was searching for something, some unknown thing that if I could just lay hold of it I would be satisfied. I would be content. I wasn't content to just sit around at home. Home was awful.

Home was not a haven where my heart was at rest. Home was turning into a monster that was seeking to devour the precious bit of self-control that I had left. I had always prided myself on my self-control; I didn't lose my composure in times of stress—well, not very often. I didn't cry out and make a fuss when my babies were born, even after all those hours of pain. I didn't lose my temper in public and make a scene. I didn't tell my family what I really thought of them when they aggravated me. I didn't get mad and blast the doctors who were always making me feel inadequate, incompetent, and insecure. No. I didn't tell the therapists how the screaming of my own child during all those hours of therapy grated on my nerves. I didn't tell them how useless all these exercises appeared to me. I didn't tell the few friends I had at the time just how I truly felt about all these things. Instead, I saved all these frustrations up in my bank of self-reserve and carried on going through the motions of living.

I wanted something, I just didn't know what. I wanted someone, but I didn't know who it was. I signed up for a course in yoga at night school, which taught me a few exercises to help me to relax and get to sleep easier. Otherwise, I wasted my time for twenty Wednesday nights. I also took a course in macramé and I started going out visiting in the evenings after Ken came in for supper. The kids would be in bed and he could babysit. At this point, Daniel was going to sleep between six and six-thirty each night and sleeping until about two a.m. Once I put Denine to sleep, she never moved from where I put her. Ken never seemed to object, so I went.

I'd drop in to visit the minister and his family. They always seemed glad to have me. I would often go to my mother's; we would sit over tea and try to out-complain each other. I'd go to home sales parties where everyone was usually nice and friendly. But the visits I enjoyed the most were to the family that had taken care of Denine that weekend a year earlier. There were six children between the ages of four and fourteen and they usually had a couple of runaway teenagers living with them. My own two younger brothers had moved in with them when they left home the year before. The house was always crowded and filled with noise. I loved it. It was a joyful noise. There was something really different about these people. Amidst all the noise and activity, the mother, Jane, radiated an inner peace that really got my attention. I just wanted to spend time in the same room as her. Sometimes I went to see them during the day, because there would always be someone there to take my two kids and play with them and love them to pieces. That was really what it was about; they loved! They just loved each other and weren't afraid to show it. They radiated love and peace, and at that time, my heart longed for both of those vital feelings. Where had the love gone from my home? Where had the peace gone?

Coming home from my nights out visiting—usually quite late—I'd often find Denine crying her little heart out. Daniel would be asleep, as would my tired and overworked husband. But little Denine would be in such a state; she'd be soaking wet and in obvious distress. Sometimes I could tell she had been crying for at least an hour, or more, by the state she was in. I'd change her, wipe her face, and cuddle her all up and tuck her in again. Once she knew I was home, she'd usually go back to sleep without any trouble.

After that, it would be time for Daniel's middle of the night feeding, and then I could sleep until six or seven, when he would be up and hungry again. I'd feed him and we'd both go back to sleep until Ken came in to make his own breakfast.

I still had trouble keeping on top of the dirty dishes. When I was younger, I had often been forced to do the dishes for my family. As a young teenager, it seemed like I *always* had to do the dishes. I'd whine and complain and procrastinate by going to the bathroom. Finally, I'd give up fighting and start washing. We were a family of ten and there were a lot of dirty dishes. Often, I'd be stuck doing them myself. My older sisters would either be out in the barn helping with the farm chores or doing homework or out on dates, and later, they were gone completely. We didn't have an indoor bathroom at the time, so everyone used the kitchen sink for washing, combing their hair, and pretty much everything else. There was a large mirror propped up in front of the sink.

At thirteen years of age, I was suddenly becoming conscious of my looks. I had long, straight brown hair, plain brown eyes, a large scar on my left eyebrow, a long skinny nose, a non-descript smile, and a pale face. I was forced to spend—literally—hours in front of that mirror, usually after crying about doing those wretched dishes, with puffy eyes and a bitter feeling. I was forced to stare at myself through all of these changing moods. When no one was around, I would start making faces at myself to see if I could improve what I was forced to look at. I came to hate my looks. Every little pimple that erupted caused me distress. The problem was that my daydreaming and staring into the mirror usually got me in trouble because I was taking too long with the dishes. Some nights I actually did finish, but never before the rest of the family came in for their usual toast and chocolate milk before bedtime, which of course only made more dirty dishes.

Now that I had my own home and family—and my own dirty dishes—I carried all of this in my heart. Only now I had no one to holler at me for not doing the dishes and there was no mirror to have to look into. Now there was only a plain gray wall, and there were always lots of dirty dishes and very few clean ones.

Ken preferred to make his own breakfast. He made only one request: that I keep at least one frying pan clean so he had something to fry his bacon and egg in. We had about six frying pans. To this day when the dishes pile up—and I am ashamed to say they still do —there is generally one clean frying pan for his use.

I decided that if I had an automatic dishwasher my dirty dish problem would be solved. Ken argued that even if I did get one, I'd still have a problem. I begged and pleaded and sulked until finally a couple of years later, he let me buy one. He was right; I still have a problem. This discovery didn't do my pride any good.

Living in the old farmhouse that we do, we've had to put up with quite a number of inconveniences. Oh, we have indoor plumbing and a nice large bathroom and all the major appliances. It's just that some of them are slightly antiquated, but as long as there was any use left in them, we had to use them or do without. Our kitchen sink was an old porcelain one with two bowls. One was shallow and the other was very deep; they were both quite wide. I used the shallow one for washing dishes and bathing babies.

Before Daniel was born, I used a portable metal rinse tub that had to be dragged into the kitchen from the back room, along with the old wringer washer. These were placed in the middle of the kitchen in such a fashion that the washing machine could be plugged into an electrical outlet and the tubs were situated so that I could wring clothes out from each of the two sections in them. These were then filled up by pail from the kitchen sink faucet. We were on a rain-fed cistern and water was in limited supply on the farm.

My back was bothering me very much in those days, especially when I was under great stress. I did laundry only once a week. I had to get Ken to fill the tubs for me, after dragging them in. Sometimes we would be short on hot water, so he would carry two pails of it in from the barn. I was allowed only one wash load and two rinse loads and I was expected to do all my laundry in this way. This is the format that was set down by Ken's mother years ago and I was expected to follow suit. The men emptied the dirty water out the next day, or the next week—whenever they got around to it. I was forbidden to dump it down the kitchen sink. Needless to say, washday became very aggravating.

Denine was getting harder and harder to feed. She made such a fuss that I found I could not eat and feed her at the same time. Up until that point, I had always tried to feed her at our usual meal times. As Daniel got bigger and started feeding himself and needed more personal attention, I put his highchair on the other side of the table near his father, forcing Ken to help him. I couldn't handle both kids at the same time. Eventually, I started feeding Denine at other times and left her in the other room watching TV while we ate. It provided some measure of peace.

Chapter 11: Depression

Depression entered my soul totally and completely in the winter of 1976. I didn't care if the housework never got done. I didn't care if the kitchen floor was only washed three or four times a year. I didn't care if I didn't have anything decent to wear. I couldn't afford to go out and buy new clothes very often, and even then, my figure did not correspond to the standard sizes available in the stores. Things either didn't fit right or they cost too much. I sewed a few things here and there and got by, if not very fashionably. At this time in my life, I had succeeded in reaching one long time goal of mine: my hair was now down to my waist. I had always wanted to have long, long hair like Rapunzle. It was easy to care for. I'd wash it once a week and forget about it the rest of the time. The only problem was that it often got in the way. Ken liked when I wore it loose, not tied up, so, it would often get wound up into the wringer. He'd roll on top of it in bed, and if I turned over I'd get scalped. Daniel was constantly pulling on it as he climbed all over me. I was pulling long hairs out of sweaters. I worked hair into the macramé I was trying to do; I really put myself into my work, as it turned out.

I was not happy. But I didn't dream of telling anybody. I had no ambition to do anything, no motivation to complete any job I started. I napped every afternoon. Eventually I started taking an extra nap in the late morning, before lunch. Then I found that I couldn't sleep well at night, so I went out more often. I read constantly to avoid reality and I had the TV on all day. It was becoming a vicious cycle.

Unless they fussed a lot, the kids were more often than not ignored. When Ken came in for meals, I would get up and start planning what to cook. I'd often thaw frozen hamburger to fry or warm up leftovers. He would be tired when he came in and would just want to lie down to rest awhile. He often watched the Flintstones to take his mind off things. To a hungry man, the smell of a meal cooking should be a wonderful thing. But to Ken, it often gave him indigestion and nausea as he was forced to wait up to a half an hour to eat. I would try to find the least dirty of the dirty plates and wash them off, and then we would eat wherever we could find room on the cluttered table.

When we were done with our main course, Ken expected dessert. Since I seldom planned meals in advance, we ate ice cream for dessert a lot. Butterscotch was his favourite and I always had some on hand. Ken was a meat and potatoes man, whereas I liked stews and soups and casseroles. He suffered through a lot of mixed-up meals and he complained very little. He just spent more time out of the house. He liked to eat his dessert in front of the television. I wanted to spend time with him, so I often followed and forgot to go back and clean off the table until the next meal. Then it would start all over again; it was a vicious, never-ending cycle.

It was around this time that my parents moved again, so I left the two children with Ken's mother and I went to supervise their move. I took some measure of comfort from getting them moved and settled in an orderly fashion. I stayed behind to clean up the mess in their old house. It was good to have some positive work to do, and to get it done on time. I went home late, tired and aching, only to find a house filled with—what else—dirty dishes and a big mess.

After my parents' move, I got more and more depressed. I'd read by the hour, or watch television from early morning until late at night, or sometimes, I'd do both at the same time—anything to escape reality. At six months old, Daniel pulled himself up to a standing position quite suddenly. I was wildly excited and had to tell everyone. I had never been able to brag about any of Denine's progress (as there had been almost none), so as time went on, I was happy to tell everyone about every new thing that my perfectly normal little boy could do. But with Daniel learning how to stand came some new problems: he'd stand up against anything he could grab, but he didn't know how to get down, so he'd start to scream for help, sometimes even at three in the morning. I'd have to get up and show him again how to get down. He was very cautious about falling.

I had been suppressing my feelings of depression for so long that I finally reached a point where I would walk through the house with my fists clenched to keep from throwing and smashing things. At the time, the one great desire of my heart was to smash every window in the house. But something kept stopping me. I knew that if I smashed the windows that would make an awful mess, which I would have to clean up, and I just couldn't bear to do that. So, I would pass by the windows with my fists clenched and go watch my soap opera.

Now the show I used to watch at the time had some pretty interesting things in it. People were cheating on their spouses. One teenage girl moved in with her boyfriend and got pregnant. Her mother arranged for an abortion after the boyfriend promised to marry her and then skipped town. He showed up in another daytime series weeks later. Everyone was rich and beautiful. No one had mountains of dirty dishes and smelly diapers. One morning I was awake at three o'clock wondering what one of the characters was going to do next. Then I realized what I was doing; I was living in a dream world that glamorized sin and spending more time worrying about that than about what was going on in my own life. After that, I deliberately shut off the TV and forced myself to leave the house from two to three o'clock every day. To this day, I abhor soap operas that give us a false view of real life.

All this time I was still taking Denine to therapy at the Cerebral Palsy Centre at Chedoke Hospital. The therapist saw that I needed a break from worrying about Denine for a while, so she suggested that I take Dan and go somewhere for an hour. I had a friend who lived two blocks away, so I spent many one-hour visits with her while Denine was in therapy. She had a little boy who played with Daniel and we had a nice time together. Other times I'd spend an hour shopping or doing some laundry at a local Laundromat. The therapist later told me that when she first offered me the hour, I just ran. I couldn't get away fast enough.

Ken was still playing hockey on Sunday nights and I still went to see him play. I often left my two babies with my in-laws, or sometimes I got a sitter. My sister Amy was still pretty young and sometimes she came over for the weekend and her friend Jeannie would come too. Now Jeannie had a special charm that I knew nothing about. She was sweet and gentle and loved to spend time with Denine. She would play an important role in our lives as the years went by. She was Jane's oldest daughter, of the family that I enjoyed spending so much time with. Amy was going through an adolescent rebellion of her own and many times she came to our place for the weekend to get away from the tensions at home with our alcoholic father. She didn't like to help with any of the work around the house, but she provided company, and in those days I seldom ever had visitors. When I did, I would be so embarrassed by the messy house that I couldn't enjoy them properly. I needed to be needed by Amy.

I wanted to die. I hated living. I hated my husband; at least, I felt no love towards him. Our physical relationship was not what it ought to have been. I thought only of myself in those days, and I did not realize the needs of my faithful husband. For he did remain faithful and true to me, even though I rejected his advances and pushed him away when he wanted to get close. I did not enjoy the physical intimacy of the act of marriage. I found it uncomfortable and irritating. Any small caress or hug from Ken was an instant invitation to go to bed. It was an all or nothing proposition, I thought; in my eyes, he was a sex maniac. What had happened to the hours we used to sit in each other's arms watching television? Why didn't we hold hands when we walked together? Where were the stolen kisses behind the door? All these things that had made our courtship so exciting were no longer there. We had been married for four and a half years. When a marriage counsellor confronted him the year before, Ken had denied that we had any problems in our relationship. He was never one to talk openly about such personal things, let alone open up to this strange, aggressive woman who was probing so deeply into intimate things. But no matter what he said, I wanted to die. I couldn't stand my life anymore. I wanted to run away and leave Ken, Denine, and Daniel behind. I didn't know where I would go, but I was determined to go.

Then I realized that I had no money, no income of my own to finance running away. Who would look after my children? Who would come and care for them? Ken was seldom home to take on that responsibility. I'd have to take the kids with me, I realized. But if I took them with me, I'd be taking the problems along with them, so I came to the conclusion that I might just as well stay home.

All this time I didn't share what I was feeling or thinking with anyone. I complained often about how my back was hurting and about Ken. I found many opportunities to tear him to pieces in front of his friends. Whenever we went out together, he would sit quietly and watch as I put him down. Afterwards, on the way home, he would give me such a tongue lashing that I would not want to speak to him for days. I was both hurt and full of guilt.

About this time, the four of us went to visit my parents one night in their new home. We weren't there twenty minutes before Ken said, "Let's go home." Denine was crying on my mom's knee, Daniel was fussing on Amy's knee, and as Ken watched, he thought that I had some nerve dumping my miserable kids on everyone else. So we went home. I was furious!

On the drive home, he asked me a simple question, "What do you think of your brother's new girlfriend?" I was suddenly faced with expressing my thoughts out loud. I didn't say anything for a couple of minutes, but Ken persisted, "Can't you answer a simple question?"

I responded in anger and suddenly something started to happen: I started telling him all the things in my heart that I had been storing up for the past two years. From eight-thirty in the evening until about two in the morning, I unloaded all of my frustrations and pains, all my disappointments and shattered hopes. I was finally finding a way to verbally express my hateful feelings and all the bitterness in my heart to the one person who really needed to know how I truly felt. It was the first time I had cried since that day two years earlier when the doctors had told us how hopelessly retarded Denine was. Ken just listened to me and was able to understand a bit. He had the good sense to be silent and let me rant instead of telling me how to fix it.

A few days later, while I was in bed reading and my sister was watching the kids, I came to a decision about what I would do. I went to Ken and demanded (I didn't ask), "I am going to England to visit my sister. You are paying for it. If you want to go along that's fine, but I am going."

He looked at me for one long minute, and then said quietly, "Okay, I'll take you to England." This was the beginning of a time of healing.

Chapter 12: Vacation at Last

We soon had reservations for a flight to England in late March. In order to get passports, we needed a guarantor, a professional that knew us to vouch for us, so together we went to our family doctor. Ken told him what he had been observing about my behaviour and lack of motivation. The doctor gave me some antidepressants. When they started to take effect, the urge to smash things went away. The need to sleep so much went away. I started taking an interest in doing things. I even started an ambitious project: I embroidered twenty-four squares with nursery rhyme characters for a quilt for Daniel. But inside, I still felt nothing. People would ask if I was excited about going to England, and I would shrug and say, "I suppose so." I was almost afraid to get excited about the trip; for fear that it wouldn't be a reality.

Before we could go on our ten-day trip, we had to get someone to look after Denine. Ken's parents were taking

Daniel, so it would not have been fair to expect them to take her as well. Then I remembered that the very first time we had attended the clinic at Chedoke, our pediatrician had said that if we ever wanted to go on holiday and needed respite care, to let them know. Up until then, going on holiday was not a part of our lifestyle. We reached out to them, and they put us in touch with the director of Dr. Rygiel's Home for Children. This home, on Whitney Avenue in West Hamilton, was a short fifteen-minute drive from our home. I hadn't even known it existed until this point. We made the necessary arrangements for a two-week stay and were told that after we came back, we should come back to inquire about getting some relief help with Denine.

The last week of March finally arrived and we took our first jumbo jet flight together to England. I had read so much about the romantic English countryside and was looking forward to visiting a real castle and manor house. I was not disappointed. We even got to pick up a few shells from the Atlantic Ocean. Ken and I took our first train ride together. During this time I found out some interesting new things about my husband; for instance, he hated shopping. Where I could spend hours and hours browsing through stores, he was content to get some groceries and get home. My oldest had gotten married the same summer as Ken and I and she and her husband had moved to England five years earlier. We had kept up a faithful correspondence over the years. They had two children and she was expecting another in the fall. We enjoyed quiet days with them and Ken and I got to spend a lot of time just being together getting reacquainted. We learned to relax in each other's company. The holiday was everything we could have hoped for.

When we came home, a more relaxed mother went to pick up Denine from Dr. Rygiel's. The director told me that when I had taken Denine in two weeks earlier, I was so uptight that she knew I needed some help. So we made arrangements for Denine to attend the home three days a week for respite care, just to see how it would work out. Each of these mornings, I would feed her breakfast and then drive her into Hamilton at around nine o'clock. The staff at Rygiel would then look after her all day and I would come back to pick her up between three-thirty and four o'clock. At Rygiel, she was put into a specialized program, designed especially for her particular needs. She had therapy and exercises. She visited the whirlpool. They fed her lunch and got her involved in many other activities.

I was advised to take my son, who was ten months old, and spend some time with him. Go out for lunch with a friend; take time to do something new; anything to get out of the rut I had allowed myself to get into. I once heard that a rut is a grave with both ends kicked out.

I got a part-time job selling a product at home parties for a few months. I spent more money than I earned, but I had a good time doing something new and challenging. I got to meet many new people, some of whom have become lasting friends. I also discovered that I enjoyed standing up in front of people and talking to them. After the initial stage fright and insecurity passed, I found that there was something I really could do. It wasn't selling products; it was talking to people. During that time, I do believe that I was being prepared for something to come later on, but I couldn't recognize it at the time. This new venture helped for a while, but it did not satisfy that longing in my heart.

Taking Denine into Rygiel each morning got to be an enjoyable routine. I would take Daniel inside with me and talk to some of the therapists to know what was going on. I wanted to see what they did with her. There was a quiet orderliness to everything that made me feel good and secure in the knowledge that my little girl was being well taken care of.

From the time I stopped nursing her at three months, Denine had always experienced constipation. It had started out as an infrequent occurrence and progressed to the point of being a chronic problem. I tried different things: corn syrup in her milk, fruit, and even laxatives, but none of these worked. She needed a laxative suppository every forty-eight hours to get her bowels to move. I would administer this at bedtime and she would have a bowel movement in the night when she was most relaxed. I would bath her in the morning and send her off to Dr. Rygiel's Home.

One day she had a bowel movement at Rygiel. Under the watchful eye of registered nurses and trained personnel, a serious problem was recognized. Up until this point, Denine was a miserable and unhappy child. She would whine and cry and, to help settle her down, I would straddle her on my knee and bounce her. What I was in fact doing was causing her distress. Because she was chronically constipated, it must have hurt her very much to be bounced on my knee in this way. The nurse recognized her problem and asked permission to administer an enmema. For a time, they did this on a regular basis in order to regulate her bowels. Then, they got her onto a liquid laxative, which was given to her daily at bedtime. It took about six weeks of this program to get her bowels functioning regularly. She became a very happy child as a result.

Had I known that the reason she cried so much could have been solved like this, I would have done something sooner. But I had not known. I was not educated in that area. Denine suddenly became a happier child who was a joy to be with. Since all of her therapy was now being done during the day and I was free of this responsibility, I too became a happier person. Life was beginning to look almost good again. Denine was going to Rygiel five days a week. We were getting into a new routine of things. The dishes were getting washed more often now—at least twice a week. It was getting a bit awkward sending cloth diapers back and forth so I started buying disposable diapers for her to use at school. As disposable diapers became more convenient, I started using them more and more on Daniel too and my wash loads started diminishing. Things were looking up.

Chapter 13: Angel Unaware

In the winter of 1976, another very significant thing happened in my life. On one of the many visits I made to Jane's house, I noticed that they had a large selection of books. Now, being the bookworm that I had always been, I could not resist browsing over the titles. None were familiar. In fact, they were rather odd titles. They dealt with things like prayer, praise, baptism, and the gifts of the Holy Spirit and Jesus. I was going to church fairly regularly at this point, and I did not recall ever hearing about topics like this. My interest was aroused and Jane asked if I wanted to read any of these books. She suggested a couple and I went home to devour these books and learn about these topics I knew nothing about.

    I read about thanking God for all the situations that come into our lives. I thought, *Thank Him? You've got to be kidding!* I was used to whining and complaining about the trials and hardships of my life. I read of people who had been healed miraculously by having hands laid on them and being prayed for. So, I laid my hands on Denine and prayed for her to be healed. Nothing happened. I read some more. I read about people who were so poor they had no money for food. They prayed for food—for red Jell-O and cake no less—and they were fed. People came to their door with the right flavour of Jell-O.

The book that got my attention the most was a small volume, only sixty-pages long. Written by Dale Evans, the wife of Roy Rogers—both childhood heroes of mine—this little book, *Angel Unaware*, opened up a whole new world of faith and belief for me. Dale and Roy had a baby girl they named Robin. Robin was very special. She had Down's syndrome. Dale shared the joys of Robin's life, but she did it in a unique way. She wrote the story from the first-person perspective of Robin herself. She was a tiny little angel on a brief pilgrimage in the Roger's home. Dale and Roy were two very special parents that God Himself had chosen to entrust this precious little baby to their care for two years.

I cried buckets of tears as I read and reread this book. I had suddenly realized that God had *chosen* me—Chris Forster—to be the mother of this very special handicapped child, Denine. God had not chosen my sisters or my friends or my neighbours; He had chosen me. He felt that I was so special that He had chosen me to be her mother. Was I ever impressed! God had chosen me! Wow—what an honour and privilege.

It would be many years before I came to realize what was happening to me at that point. But right then, it was enough to know that God had known all along what was going on in my life. I believed and accepted His plan for my life. Doors suddenly started to open. Having read so much about God and how He was working in the lives of people today, I was beginning to build up a faith of my own. One day I ventured to suggest to Ken that perhaps if we prayed for Denine, God would heal her. He responded in anger and disbelief, and I was too new in my new faith to face it, so I thought to myself, *See if I share with you again.* And until his own salvation four years later, I did not speak another single word to him of my faith or of the Lord.

Chapter 14: Surgery

In the fall of 1976, several more doors opened up for me. With Denine going to Dr. Rygiel's five full days per week, I had much more time to myself—and to spend with my small son. Daniel was walking now and there was so much that he wanted to do and get into. I allowed him to get away with everything because I was so proud of what he could do. He was so normal. I was building up a lot of guilt in my heart because I was spending more time with Daniel and enjoying it more than the time I spent with Denine.

I was finding it difficult to take both children to church with me when I went alone. Ken went quite regularly, but as winter was drawing near and the cows were in the barn all day, he had extra chores to do. Many Sundays I went alone with Daniel and left Denine at home with her dad. The sound of the old organ would cause her to start screaming. Some songs would cause her to pout and start to cry. Was she becoming sensitive to sounds? I didn't know. Daniel was learning how to talk, but he could not say "Denine." He started to call her "Dee Dee" or "Deedlee".

As Denine grew taller, she started to develop more problems with her limbs. Her arms were still held rigidly and crossed over her body. Her legs were getting longer and more spindly. She was outgrowing her special chair and we knew that some adjustments were necessary. Another seating clinic was arranged and they made some changes to her chair. She was turning more and more to the left and her body was beginning to get slightly twisted. I had to leave the chair behind for a week to have an adjustable headrest added to it.

In the meantime, we had another clinic arranged for us at the Family Practice Unit of Chedoke. There was a new doctor there among the therapists and doctors we usually had. Ken did not go with me to these appointments anymore. This time, an orthopaedic surgeon examined her. During his examination, there were a few students present. He stripped off all her clothes and held her out before them like a specimen, like nothing more than a hunk of meat. I was so angered by his cold, impersonal manner. It seemed like I did not exist as anyone of importance either. He was the teacher, and Denine was a rare object for him and his students to scrutinize. It was awful! Didn't he realize that she was my baby? That she was bone of my bone, flesh of my flesh? Did he not realize that she was a live human being created in the image of God?

I was informed that in order to facilitate diapering, she would require surgery to sever the muscles in the upper part of her legs. At three years of age, Denine was able to hold her urine for a number of hours, and when she released it, it was like a flood. Double diapering was necessary, but the second diaper would not remain in place. Her hip joints were slipping out of their sockets and the scissor effect of her legs was making it exceedingly difficult to dress her properly. Surgery was arranged for early January.

I left this clinic angered and upset. I still had to go pick up her chair at the other side of the hospital. I hadn't been able to park close to the door and I had to carry Denine across the hospital, only to find that the chair wasn't ready. I got back into my truck and just sat there and cried. I felt like nobody cared.

At the end of November, we were informed that Denine had been accepted into a program at the Child Development Centre (CDC) on Leeming Street in Hamilton. Our therapist and two girls from the CDC came to our house one day for an interview and assessment. As we sat in the parlour and tried to talk, Denine whined and made a fuss. Her head would sometimes slip off the headrest and have to be adjusted. At one point, I deliberately got up and left the room for a few minutes. Once I was gone, she settled down quietly and paid attention to her visitors. When I came back, the whining and noises resumed. If I picked her up, she would quiet down. The ladies found it interesting to observe.

We made specific arrangements for her entrance into this new school program. A bus would come to our house everyday at eight a.m. to pick Denine up, and it would bring her home before five p.m. every night. It would be a long day for her, but they would allow for a nap. She was entered into this new program only a few days before her big surgery, which gave the staff at the CDC just enough time to see the before and after results of the operation.

Denine on couch with A-frame cast

When she came home from the hospital after her surgery, Denine had an A-frame leg cast, which meant that she had a cast on each leg, held together by a bar between her ankles. This made it very awkward to handle her. The only clothing she could wear over her casts was overalls with dome snaps. I put booties or socks on her toes. In order to change her diaper, I had to be careful not to get moisture down inside the plaster. There were plastic bags taped to the top of the casts and waterproof dressings on her stitches. She was unable to sit up in her chair, so I would lay her on the couch with pillows so she could see what was going on. The cast remained on for five weeks. We went back to McMaster to have them removed, and how the sound of that saw cutting off the plaster irritated my nerves! I didn't understand how he could remove that thing without cutting her, but he did. She had developed two pressure sores from the cast: a small one and another larger one. They soon healed up.

January, 1977

Medical Observations: Orthopaedic Clinic:

-*because of marked adductor rigidity of her extremities and contracture at the hips, we felt she should have soft tissues releases in order to make her care easier*

-*had soft tissue releases of both hips carried out one month ago*

-*this required extensive release of all of the medial soft tissues, including division of the adductors, the spectator nerve, the iliopsoas muscle, and the origin of the hamstrings at the ischial tuberosity*

-*in addition, the medical capsule of the hip joint was divided*

-*with this extreme division, reasonable abduction of the hip could be obtained*

-*she was immobilized in abduction casts*

-*casts were removed and operative wounds healed*

-*her hips are in reasonably good position after the treatment*

-*requires no other orthopaedic treatment at this time*

-*will see her again at the Orthopaedic Clinic at Chedoke when scheduled for a review in a month or two*

Chapter 15: Child Development Centre

Denine soon settled into the routine of the new school program. Now that a bus picked her up and brought her home each day, I was released from making twice daily trips into Hamilton.

I joined a program for mothers with small children, at a nearby church. The mothers met every Wednesday morning and visited over coffee while the preschoolers were involved in an organized play and craft time. The mothers took turns making coffee and babysitting and it was wonderful! As Denine started going to the CDC regularly, I started taking Daniel, who was one and a half years old at this time, to Playtime at this church. He had an opportunity there to play with other children for the first time, and it was then that he started showing the first signs of a serious behavioural problem.

I was finally in a place where I could start acting like a normal mother with a normal child and do normal things with other normal mothers. We often did crafts together or held Tupperware parties. We took the kids to the fire station or to the farm. The mothers met once a month or so for a movie or a night of shopping; once, we went to the art gallery. We had meetings and even a party once in a while. It was great, but still, it did not satisfy the longing in my heart.

One Wednesday morning we were having a Christmas party for the children. I had to bring Denine that day. She sat in her chair off to the side, watching the other children run around and play. For the past two years, she had been around other handicapped children continuously. It was interesting to watch her watch the normal children playing. I found out later that one mother in particular noticed what was going on and longed to speak to me, to ask me how I was able to cope with this special child. She herself had just found out that her only child, a girl, had an incurable problem and she didn't know where to turn or who to talk to. She didn't speak to me about it until several years later, when her daughter and my son started school together, and by then she had found a way to cope. Looking back, what could I have said to her then? I didn't have any concrete answers on how to cope, even for myself.

Chapter 16: I Want Another Baby

During that winter of 1977, my heart was again longing for something that I could not describe. I entered a class to learn how to swim. At the grand old age of twenty-five, I was terrified of the water. I could not even bear to be splashed. We had a swimming pool at the farm at the time and I was a horrid spoilsport. I learned to overcome my fear of swimming by learning how *not to drown*, but I never really learned how to *swim*. This did not satisfy my soul either.

I decided, without really consulting my husband on the issue, that what we needed was another baby. So I planned and I plotted, and soon enough, Ken granted me permission. So I set out to get pregnant. I must add that he delighted in this because it meant that we were spending more time together and learning more about each other's physical and sexual needs. Six months passed before I saw any indications of approaching motherhood. Those were the happiest six months we had had in years.

We discovered that I was to give birth the following July, and around the same time, something else came along that shattered the peaceful times we were having. It happened innocently enough. I was in the early stages of pregnancy and was beginning to experience nausea and other symptoms. One day at suppertime, Daniel decided that he would wash his own hands. His daddy had taught him how to sit atop the laundry hamper at the bathroom sink and wash his own hands. So, my two and a half year old son locked the bathroom door, pulled up the laundry hamper, and climbed onto it. Sitting down oh so nicely, he put the stopper in the sink drain, and then he turned the tap on—full blast. Being right handed, he turned on the cold water tap. By the time we realized what was going on, there was an inch of water on the bathroom floor and he was screaming hysterically. Ken had to break the door lock in order to rescue him, and I got to clean up the mess. I was so mad at my little boy that I spanked him and put him in his crib to keep him out of trouble. He was so upset in return that he climbed right out for the first time and followed me back to the kitchen. And thus began a battle of wills that would carry on for many years.

I tried everything I could think of to keep him in his crib. In desperation, I even tried tying him to the crib with a bathrobe belt, untying him once he had fallen asleep. This proved to be a big mistake because it was the beginning of night terrors for the child. He started having serious temper tantrums. My in-laws were pressuring me to toilet train him, but I didn't have any idea how to do it. Daniel would just take off his diapers; he preferred to go without. Putting him to bed became yet another battle of wills to see who could outlast the other. There were many nights when he fell asleep on the floor by my bed and I carried him to his own. Other times he'd climb right into our bed and keep us both awake until he was sleeping.

I decided that the best thing to do was to put him into a big bed of his own and lie down with him. As I grew in size with the new baby, I realized that this pregnancy was different than my other two. I carried this baby low and had a great deal of pain and discomfort walking and standing. The doctor said I had a hernia. My back troubled me constantly and I was able to do very little work. I was overweight and sluggish. I needed a nap every day now from sheer exhaustion. I could not let Daniel out of my sight or he would get into mischief; I didn't dare fall asleep unless he was asleep first. I managed to get him to lay down on the couch with me for his naps. At night I would have to lie down on his bed for up to an hour until he settled down to sleep. Ken would either be in bed or on the couch asleep, and I could not join him until Daniel was safely asleep. All this time, Denine would lie there quietly and watch. She would never sleep until there were no people left around for her to watch. This routine proved the most annoying when we would have company.

In January there were several bad snowstorms. One particular morning, it was raining heavily when we got up and I sent Denine off to school as usual. By late morning, the rain had turned to snow and the winds were up to eighty miles an hour. In the afternoon, I discovered a snowdrift in the downstairs bedroom. The high winds were forcing snow through a breathing hole in the old storm window and it was all over the carpet and drapes. I bundled up, took a small towel in hand, and went outside. I had to hug the wall as I worked my way into the wind around the other side of the house to stop up the hole. Coming back was quicker as the wind drove me along the wall. When I reached the porch, there was my son, boots on, heading out to get me. If he had taken two steps off that porch, the winds would have carried him away and we may not have found him until springtime! The roads were all closed by noon and many people were stranded at work or school overnight. Since Denine had gone to school that morning as usual, that is where she ended up spending the night. They were able to get most of the other children home early in the day, but we lived too far out of town.

So, the two teachers and Denine spent a day and a half together. It helped the teachers get to know more about Denine's peculiarities. For example, Denine would not relax to go to sleep if there was anyone else around. She had to keep her eyes on all of the action. That night, because they didn't know this, one of them tried to sleep with her on the couch in the staff room. Needless to say, they remained awake most of the night.

By ten o'clock that night the winds and snow had stopped, leaving behind much destruction and snow and very little activity. Our phone was out and the house started getting cold. On investigation, we found the furnace downstairs was completely buried under a blanket of snow that had blown in through a broken window. Ken went across the road to the neighbours to get help, only to find that among the six vehicles that were in the ditch by our laneway, was a furnace repairman who was waiting to find a way home. He gladly fixed the furnace at no charge. I think he was an angel in disguise. The next day was spent ploughing out the lane and the roads. It was late afternoon before I could get out to pick up Denine.

January, 1978

Medical Observations: Denine's therapist's experience and perspective of that night.

Bundled Denine up and decided to drive her home. We got two blocks from the school and sat in traffic unable to go anywhere. I was on the verge of panic. How would I carry this awkward-sized girl back to the school to safety through the deepening snow? What if I were pregnant or had a second child with me? How do mothers cope in emergencies like this? How do mothers cope in nice weather, carrying or lifting or dragging, whatever the case may be, their retarded child up two flights to their small apartment? I suddenly had a great deal of compassion and admiration for the many mothers who take all of this in stride in daily and continue coping. I was able to get back to the school safely to spend the night in warmth and protection.

Chapter 17: Can't You Help Me?

Denine was born with a small cyst above her lip. It was a small lump under the skin that would turn white when she cried. That winter, it started to discharge a bit of pus when she had her bottle. In spite of all the therapy and work they had been doing with her around feeding, I persisted in bottle-feeding most of her meals at home. It was too time-consuming and too frustrating for me to wait for her to eat some solid food; she spit most of it out anyway.

As I sat with her in the rocking chair, feeding her from a bottle, I noticed a bit of pus coming out of her cyst. If I pressed the rim of the bottle to the edge of the cyst, more would ooze out. Something inside me caused me to keep on pressing. After a few weeks of doing this off and on, an infection started to develop and more pus oozed out more often. The teachers at school noticed one day and we called the pediatrician. An infection had set in and a saline bath was requested to help clean and drain it. Denine was put on antibiotics and we were sent off to see a plastic surgeon.

I'll never forget the day we went to see this particular doctor. He was another new doctor on the list of the many professionals we saw. His office was in an old medical building in downtown Hamilton, just off James Street South. There are many professional buildings in this area and very few parking lots. It was the middle of February and we had just had another heavy snowfall. Fortunately, I had left Daniel with someone the day of our appointment. As I drove up to the building, surrounded by one-way streets, I discovered the parking lot was completely full. There were some spots on the street, but anywhere vacant was filled with snow. Eventually, I found a place to park my pick-up truck four blocks away.

I hugged my precious nineteen pound bundle of girl and snowsuit close to me, diaper bag and purse slung over my protruding belly, through snow drifts, around cars, across streets, and finally into the elevator that took us up six floors. In the doctor's office, we sat and waited the usual hour.

But this doctor was different. He was noticeably shocked at Denine's appearance. He was quite young as doctors go, and he was obviously intrigued by my little girl. Having completed his examination and asked all the appropriate questions, he stated quite emphatically, "It's amazing that she has lived this long."

I had never looked at the matter from that perspective before. Surgery was scheduled for early April, after the infection had had time to be controlled.

By the time I got home from seeing the plastic surgeon that day, I was wiped right out. Denine was having surgery again, and who cared if I was tired or my back hurt or I was frustrated. Who cared if I was gaining too much weight and could hardly walk with the hernia and the baby weighing heavily inside? Who cared that it was getting harder and harder to carry Denine anywhere?

My dryer broke down once and for all. It was winter and I had no place to dry all my clothes. So I started packing them into garbage bags, going to Brantford to my mother's, and spending the day doing laundry. She would usually finish it and I would pick it up the next day.

Daniel came down with a mild case of chicken pox. He had only a few pox, and those were not too itchy. But Denine had to stay home in quarantine. As the chicken pox faded from Daniel's body, the baby bonus cheque arrived and I took him shopping one spring-like day in late March. He needed new shoes, but worse still, we needed a new toaster. We went to the mall first to find little boy's shoes in extra wide size. They didn't have any. So we went over to Consumer's to get a toaster, but they couldn't cash the cheque. Se we had to go back to the mall to cash the cheque. As was his custom, Daniel took off down the mall when I let go of him to do up my coat. I was tired and frustrated and in a hurry. So, instead of chasing him clear to the end of the mall, I ran the few steps and grabbed the little brat! I was to regret this many times in the weeks to come, as I pulled a muscle in my lower back. I still had to go back for the toaster, then downtown to a specialty shoe store. We did eventually get home, after a while.

By the time I got supper dealt with and was putting the kids to bed, I could hardly walk. I was unable to even climb the stairs; I was so tired and so worn out. We'd missed our nap that afternoon. My back hurt so much. Daniel was so disobedient. Then he started demanding a drink of water, demanding to go pee. The bathroom was downstairs. The bedrooms were upstairs. I'd had enough. I just sat down on the stairs and started to cry. Ken yelled at me, "Take the kid to the bathroom already and keep him quiet!"

"I can't do it," I cried. "I can't even climb the stairs; I'm in so much pain. Can't you help me?" Ken took Daniel to the bathroom, the first of many trips they would take together. We got someone to look after the kids and Ken took me to the doctor. He diagnosed a sprained back and I was told to get lots of rest and to take 282's for the pain. *What about the children? How can I run after a two and a half year old that keeps going? How can I cook meals for the family? And Denine is home on quarantine for two more weeks!* My thoughts were roiling in panic. The doctor told us, "Get someone to come in and help. What about your fourteen-year-old sister? She just got her tonsils out and is off school for two weeks. Get her to come over. She just has to keep from talking."

So, Amy came to stay for two weeks and looked after Daniel and Denine. I got some books from the library and lay flat on my back and just read. The kids stayed in front of the TV most of the time. Spring had arrived and outside was all mud. I took two 282's as needed and went to see a chiropractor three times a week for a while. That helped enough to bear the pain. After three weeks or so I was able to get around, but I drew the line at carrying Denine to the bus. There was so much mud in our yard that the bus was unable to get up to the house, so we put Denine and her chair into a wagon and pulled her across the yard to the bus. Denine did not get the chicken pox and went back to school. Amy went back home and Ken came in early each morning to carry Denine and her chair out to the bus. Peace came for a few days.

The infection had gone away and Denine once again entered the hospital for surgery. The procedure was simple. They made a small cut above the cyst, removed it and put in two tiny stitches to close it, then covered it with a Band-Aid. She remained in the hospital only a few days. Her father had to go with her to take her in, and later, to carry her home. We argued most of the way there and all the way home. We were to keep the stitches clean for a few days and make a return trip to the surgeon's office. This time there was one parking place in the lot and we only had to walk one block. Why did things always work out so simply when Ken was there? I would have all sorts of problems and frustrations when I went alone, and when he came to help, it all ironed out. I didn't understand. I still don't.

Perhaps things might have worked out better in those days if he had been able to be with me through the appointments and the therapy sessions and everything else. But he had a farm to run and it was more important than anything going on within the jurisdiction of the house. That was my domain. So, I ran it the way I wanted to and I didn't like the way it was working out.

One consolation I did have that spring was a brand new portable dishwasher that was supposed to solve my dirty dish problem forever. But it was usually in the way and there were too many dishes to do up in one load. And since we were on a rain-fed cistern, we ran out of water often.

1978: Child Development Centre

Medical Observations: Motor Skills

GROSS - Denine can move her head from side to side while lying in a prone or supine position. She lifts and momentarily supports her head when on an adult's shoulder. Denine lifts her head forward from a tilted-back position. She holds her head erect when lifted from supine for one or two seconds. She can lift her head off a mat when over a bolster. She can turn from her side to her stomach after being rolled from her back to her side. Denine's legs are bending at the knee less than the forty-five degrees she was able to bend them at time of last report. All of Denine's limbs and muscles are tighter. She no longer bends when put in the car seat but tends to lie flat against the chair. All exercises are still being done to maintain some movement in the limbs.

FINE - Denine will tolerate having her hands opened. When her fingers are pried open, her hand will close around an object (this closure is involuntary). She will glance momentarily at the object. Denine's sight follows past midline only by moving her head. Denine watches a moving object at a distance of two to three feet. She watches the smoke from an extinguished candle. Upon occasion, Denine has moved her arms to knock over a tower of blocks, but this movement may have been involuntary.

Medical Observations: Denine's Self-Help Skills

FEEDING - Denine will tolerate having some liquid in her mouth and she will swallow. She drinks from a regular cup without a spout. The cup is held tightly to Denine's lips and tilted slowly. After several seconds, Denine starts to swallow. Occasionally Denine will continue *to gulp even after she has taken all the liquid. It is almost like once she starts the pattern, it takes a second or two to stop. Denine eats regular food cut into bite-sized pieces. She can move the food about in her mouth with her tongue. She has a tongue thrust but still manages to use her tongue to pull some of the food back into her mouth. She has trouble eating creamy foods like ice cream, pudding, and gravy. Although Denine's mouth closes on the spoon, it sometimes opens again involuntarily, and so she does lose some food. Denine chews her food, but because she becomes lazy at times, she will swallow larger pieces.*

DRESSING/TOILETING - Denine is totally dependent in both of these areas. She co- operates passively while being dressed or undressed. She makes no indication of having soiled her diaper.

Chapter 18: Can We Pray With You?

That spring, our minister was ordained and he and his family were making plans to move to Newfoundland at the end of June. I had visited their home often in the previous two years and I would miss them. With their departure would come a new student minister. Terry Somerville and his wife Karen were still on their honeymoon. That fall, both of them would be in university full time and we were eagerly awaiting their arrival. The whole church made plans for a luncheon following the first service that he would lead.

Ken went alone to that service with Daniel, because I was unable to go. Something more important had come up; Denine was sick. Again. Only this time it was different. I don't recall just why or how she started vomiting, but vomit she did. Everything that entered her stomach was rejected. She even started throwing up plain water, which meant that she was getting dehydrated. I don't recall that she ran a fever, but she was getting weaker, and worst of all, she was losing weight. One month before her fifth birthday, she weighed nineteen and a half pounds. One week later she was down to sixteen pounds.

I took Denine into Emergency on Friday. As I carried her in, I met one of the ladies from our church at the receptionist desk. She asked if I had come in to have my baby. The baby had settled into delivery position three weeks earlier, but I still had three weeks to go by the calendar. But the specialist, who I was seeing every Thursday, had told me the day before that it could be anytime now. But that wasn't the reason for my visit; I was here for Denine.

Denine with Mom and Dad

We were assigned to a doctor who turned us over to another—very young—doctor, who proceeded to examine this rare specimen of humanity (Denine) of whom he was slightly afraid. Her legs were quite brittle and one cracked rather loudly during his examination. He was worried that her leg had broken; it had not. He decided that a spinal tap was needed.

Among the many complications and physical problems that Denine had was a curved spine. Not being the least bit knowledgeable about such things, I was very little help. He finally gave up and called for assistance. The original doctor came with a nurse and they proceeded to do another spinal tap, only to find that no problems were indicated there. Our pediatrician was away and these professional people had never seen Denine before, and therefore they were not familiar with any of her problems or needs.

Why had the original doctor left us in the hands of the inexperienced intern? It would have saved my girl much distress. An intravenous was arranged and she was admitted to the children's ward. The next morning, I left Daniel with my sister in Dundas and went back to the hospital to see Denine. She had swollen right up from the intravenous and looked rather plump. They said she could go home if I had some clothes for her. So I went back to my sister's to pick up a diaper and clothes from Daniel's diaper bag, and then I came back to the hospital. I had to pay the underground parking fees twice that morning.

After picking Daniel up, we got home around lunchtime. While I was getting Denine settled in the house, Daniel was carried in from the shed and I was told he'd eaten some rat poison. I phoned the poison control centre and then had to make a third trip to the hospital that day, this one much more hastily. It was a hot day and Daniel fell asleep on the drive down. We arrived at Emergency for the second time in two days. They moved quickly when I told them that my son had eaten rat poison. They pumped his stomach and found no sign of the poison. He must have spat it out earlier.

So I was left wondering why only the day before, when I had taken my profoundly handicapped daughter in with severe dehydration, the hospital staff had ho-hummed around and passed us from expert to expert. And the next day, when I took my perfectly normal son, suspected of eating rat poison, into that same hospital, the same experts had flown into action. I was too tired and pregnant to think about it too much.

So as it turned out, I missed the first church service led by our new student minister, Terry Somerville. I did make it out to the second Sunday service, a week later, with Denine in tow. Ken took Daniel in hand. As we were making our way out the door we stopped for the traditional handshake, "Good morning, how are you" routine, we were greeted with, "Is this your child? Oh, can we pray with you?" I gave permission to the lady, the new minister's mother, and she gathered Denine in her arms. Then, right there on the church steps in front of everybody, blocking the doorway, she prayed for our little girl—*out loud*. Ken was so embarrassed he just wanted to run. And that's just what he did: to find Daniel, who had run off again.

She prayed for a special blessing and she prayed for healing. She talked to God Himself. She talked as if she really knew Him! And she really meant what she was saying. I'd never met anyone like this before! Oh, I had read about them a few years before, but to meet a real live Christian who talked to God was incredible, and I was sure that He listened. This was the beginning of a close relationship that has grown stronger as the years have gone by. What I did not know, until much later, was that this woman had a very special ministry working with handicapped children. But God knew, and He directed her to me right then when I needed it most. She never saw Denine again.

July, 1978: Child Development Centre

Medical Observations: Language

> We are still trying to teach Denine to use facial expressions as a way of communicating. Some days Denine will indicate a preference by responding with a smile, but still some days she uses no expressions at all. We have tried to encourage Denine to attend to an object and to introduce her to the names of some familiar objects, such as bowls, spoons, sweaters, toys, and clowns. Denine is taken into a room, given an object, and told the name of the object, and then each object is talked about. Some days, only one object is introduced. As yet Denine's response to this has been inconsistent. At times she appears to be listening, and at other times she cries for no reason. These exercises are to encourage Denine to point with her eyes, as well as to teach her about her surroundings. Her attention span is still very short so each session is about five to ten minutes.
>
> *Socialization:* Denine is very uneasy when approached by any of the other children in the group. She tends to cry if they try to touch her. She enjoys attention from adults when she is sure that they are not going to do exercises with her. When Denine cries, she is taken to isolation until she stops, and then she is brought back into the roll. She likes to have us sing good morning to her and she likes the attention of having the action songs done with her; however, if we sing without giving her attention, she will cry.

Chapter 19: Melanie Crystal

The time when my third baby would be born was drawing nearer. I felt like I'd been pregnant for twelve years, I was so big. I weighed far more than ever before, at 170 pounds. It was getting more and more difficult to get around. I was unable to sleep for more than an hour or two at a time. As my due date drew nearer, we had arranged for Denine to go back to the house on Charleton Avenue for two weeks while I was in the hospital. She would be taken straight from school to the home on the appointed day.

At this time, she had been getting a bit better. She was eating again. But her face was distressful to look at! Only days earlier she had swollen up so plump from the IV, and now she was so shrivelled and wrinkled. She had lost a precious three pounds—three pounds she could not afford to lose. We had one last seating clinic that spring and a whole new chair was designed for her. Her limbs had been getting progressively stiffer and more bent. Her body continued to twist more to the left than ever before, and her head was twisting the opposite way, to the right. It was becoming more difficult to hold her on my lap. My arm could not hold her erect for more than a few minutes. After that long weekend she spent in the hospital, she went back to school for about a week, and they found that she was so weak from her illness that she could not take part in her program properly. We decided to send her only for half days until she regained her strength. A visit to the pediatrician later in the week revealed that her health was so precarious that not only was school out of the question, but also the house on Charleton Avenue would not be able to provide adequate care. So, it was arranged that she would enter Dr. Rygiel's home for the next three weeks, until after the baby came.

Denine went to Rygiel with her clothes and her special chair while I sat at home to wait for this baby. In the nights leading up to my third child's birth, I felt many false labour pains. What did they call them? Oh yes, *Braxton Hicks*. The weather got progressively hotter and I just got fatter. I gained ten pounds in those last three weeks. But during that time, the most wonderful thing also happened; just in time for his third birthday, Daniel became toilet trained—finally!

We made one last visit to the obstetrician. Both Daniel and I had caught an awful virus, and I was four days overdue, sick, and fat. I pleaded with him to induce labour. I even took my packed bag to the appointment with me, hoping that he would. He admitted me into the hospital just before lunch.

At two p.m. he came by and broke my water sac. A few hours later, I went into full labour. In the meantime, Ken stayed busy; he took Daniel home, left him with his parents, milked the cows, and came back to the hospital. Unlike with my previous labours, the hospital now allowed fathers to stay past 8 p.m. Ken arrived at about eight-thirty. He didn't want to be in the delivery room, but I'd warned the doctor and the nurses not to let him get away with that.

After five hours of easy labour, Melanie Crystal made her appearance (in the presence of her father) rather abruptly into the world. She came so quickly that she'd been bathed, weighed, and named before the doctor even arrived at 10:20 p.m. on July 20, 1978. It was the hottest day of the year.

One of the greatest joys that a woman will ever experience is the safe birth of a long awaited baby. Joy filled my soul; I was so happy. From the beginning, Melanie was Daddy's little girl.

Because I had this awful virus at the time, I found it exceedingly difficult to draw a breath to cough properly, and as a result, I had to wear a facemask when I nursed my little girl. Daniel was not even allowed *near* the new baby; he was even sicker than his mother. But at least I didn't have to worry about that for five days, because his dad was looking after him.

My birthday arrived four days after the baby was born, and lo and behold, that was the only day in all the days I'd been in the hospital that my husband did not come to see me. No one came to see me all day. I was so depressed! My brother did show up after nine p.m. that night for a few minutes to bring me a beautiful box of chocolates from my mother-in-law. She never forgets. Bless her.

We brought Melanie home the next day into an incredibly dirty house that had been closed up tight against the summer heat. There were dirty dishes everywhere. You couldn't tell what colour the floor was supposed to be and the air was muggy. I carried my new baby, still wrapped in all her sterile hospital garb, down the hall to lay her in the crib in the spare room. Halfway down the hall, Daniel started coughing—or at least he tried to draw a breath to cough. He turned red in the face, finally got the cough to come, and then threw up on the carpet and collapsed in exhaustion. What had I come home to? Ken and his family all went out that night to a special Guernsey function and I had the privilege of spending my first evening home from the hospital alone, with a very hungry baby and a very sick little boy. I wept.

I didn't realize how hungry Melanie was until I tried feeding her. I had nursed the other two so I knew how to do this, but something wasn't right. My nipples were cracked and bleeding, and they hurt, oh so much! She was so hungry she just attacked. This agony continued off and on for hours, until I was in tears of pain and fatigue and frustration. Melanie was howling in hunger. Ken finally came home, took his little girl in his arms, and rocked her to sleep so nicely. We both slept for a couple of hours and tried it again, and then again . . . and again. I finally went to the doctor and told him our problem; he said to try pushing fluids for a week. He gave me formula, after I demanded it.

While we were in the hospital, Melanie had had supplemental feedings. Now, at home, she was starving. It took two days for the soreness to go away from my breasts. There had been no milk at all. The joy of bottle-feeding was that she slept through the night. The disappointment was that I didn't get to hold and cuddle her as much as I had the other children.

Chapter 20: I Didn't Know!

We brought Denine home from Rygiel at the end of July. The first three weeks of August were always allocated for staff holidays. This meant that I would look after her for three whole weeks by myself. I was not thrilled. Daniel was still coughing badly. He would often whoop for long, dreadful minutes in his sleep, and then hold his breath for eons. I would lay awake in the next room holding my own breath, willing him to breathe. Sometimes he would start to rant and rave after a coughing spell. He would have tantrums, and these become more frequent. He seemed to have them more often in the night now, usually after wetting his bed. Melanie initially required two feedings in the middle of the night, and then she only needed one, and finally, she would sleep through the night. Denine was the only one of my children who could spend a quiet night. Once asleep, she slept peacefully all through the night. In the morning, her bed would be drenched and her diaper would be soiled, but that was routine.

As I lay awake for hours every night that summer, I would listen to each child sleeping in the next room and pray for each one. I was worried that Daniel would suffocate in his whooping, that Melanie would die a crib death, and that only Denine would remain. These thoughts did not enter my mind in the daytime; I only thought about it in the middle of the night. Because she gave us the least amount of hassle in those days, Denine was ignored the most. She seemed happy just to be home all the time. She was fed and changed and in the same room as us; that's all she seemed to need. Daniel got most of his attention from being bad. Melanie was everyone's favourite; after all, she was the newest toy around, so she got lots of attention and doting. Amy came to stay with us for most of the summer to help with the new baby. To this day, Melanie adores her favourite auntie—probably because she spent so much time with her in those days.

The three weeks of staff vacation were finally over and Denine was sent off to school with her diaper bag and brand new chair. After she returned to school, we received a phone call late in the morning from the Child Development Centre.

They said, "Could you come right away? Denine has a very nasty sore on her hip. You better call the pediatrician."

I called our pediatrician, gathered the two kids, and we hurried down to the city. Denine did indeed have a very mean-looking pressure sore on her left hip, and I hadn't even known. I had bathed her and dressed her and changed her diapers, and I hadn't even noticed. Because her body was so twisted, the affected hip couldn't be seen unless she was turned completely over onto her face. Her body was shaped liked an L and she wouldn't stay on her face; she always fell back onto her back. She had been so good all month that I had ignored her to the point of cruelty. Boy, did I ever feel guilty!

The pediatrician had not seen her since early June and was not prepared for her drastically changed appearance. We tried several different measures to ease the pressure of the sore, but nothing worked. It was located in the diaper area and she couldn't lay on her other side. They considered hospitalization, but decided instead that she should be accepted into Dr. Rygiel's for nursing care, for as long as was necessary.

In September, Denine was admitted into Dr. Rygiel's for nursing care, until the sore on her hip could heal. That very first day as they were getting her dressed, she had a bowel movement, and something I'd never seen before happened: a large portion of her bowel came out as she soiled her diaper. Fortunately, the medical staff was able to calmly take things in hand. They repeatedly pushed the bowel back in, and finally they taped the opening to keep it in. What an initiation.

A week later the pediatrician called and requested an interview with my husband and me. We knew it was serious. Instinctively, we both knew that she was going to talk about a placement for Denine. Were we prepared to face this? We had agreed to not discuss the matter years earlier because we were unable to face the issue. Was this indeed why she called us? Ken had not been asked to any of the other clinics or appointments, until now.

The appointed day came and we arrived at the office, minus our other children, for once. We spoke with the doctor at length about Denine's struggles. We talked in detail about her feeding programs and about my failure to get her to eat properly. We discussed all the aspects of her nursing care to date. And so for the first time in five years of constant doctors, appointments, specialists, hospitals, therapists, and experts, I broke down and cried as I finally shared the guilt and frustration I'd been feeling over my failure to care for Denine adequately. Our pediatrician expressed compassion for me and for our struggles.

After all this, she dropped a bomb on us; a bed had become vacant at Dr. Rygiel's Home for Children. The staff had asked for permission to explore the possibility of admission to that facility for Denine. They asked if we were agreeable to a permanent placement. Denine was currently occupying this bed for temporary nursing care. As long as she was occupying that bed, no one else could come in on a permanent placement. They went on to explain that they didn't know how long she would need such nursing care, and so they could not make plans for another child. This meant that even though we hadn't even been on the waiting list, Denine was automatically placed at the top of the list for placement. As her physical disabilities were becoming increasingly more difficult to manage, the doctors felt that she would be appropriately placed within this institution. The necessary steps were taken.

I didn't quite understand the logistics of all this, but it became perfectly clear to me that Denine was now a permanent resident of Dr. Rygiel's Home for Children. It would be nearly four months before she was well enough to visit us at home.

Many of these details were unknown to us until we started doing research through our medical records for the purpose of writing this story. Why did the doctors not tell us about everything that was going on? They may have been trying to spare us further pain by withholding information, but as a result, we became fearful of what we did not know.

Chapter 21: Placement

I still could not quite understand how Denine had come to be a permanent resident of Dr. Rygiel's. It was something that Ken and I had avoided discussing for four years because it was just too painful, and suddenly it had happened without us taking any steps towards it. But as we discussed what the doctors had said, I felt a sudden peace in my heart at the thought of placing Denine in a home. Somehow I just knew that the time had come, and suddenly and unexpectedly, I felt peace about the whole thing.

Melanie was baptized that Thanksgiving Sunday. We hosted my entire family and Ken's entire family for Thanksgiving dinner and we had many family photos taken. Denine was missing. In order to make the necessary arrangements for the baptism, I took Daniel and Melanie to the new minister's house for the first of many visits. They were so pleased to have some company. Karen fell madly in love with

Melanie and tolerated Daniel out of politeness and respect for me. Our whole family adopted them as our dearest friends, and even now, they remain Auntie Karen and Uncle Terry.

One day as Karen was visiting, I told her about Denine and we went together to see her. This visit was kind of fun because someone was actually interested in what I was doing. Daniel started throwing a ball around, and when it bounced off the chair of one of the boys in a wheelchair, he started laughing. The lady on duty thought it was marvellous to have some "normal" children come in to play. It was very beneficial to the handicapped kids.

Melanie crawled around the floor and all over Denine. She had no teeth yet, but she was chewing everything in sight. She chewed "Deedlee's" fingers and kissed her face. This made Denine laugh, which was good to see for very little made her laugh in those days. Karen started praising me for what a marvellous job I'd been doing with her and I wondered where she had gotten such ideas. I'd been feeling like such a failure.

Denine was coming home for Christmas for two days, and I had looked forward to it for weeks. My child was coming home for Christmas, and I was so glad. I plotted and planned, and eventually succeeded in talking my parents into coming to our house for the traditional Christmas Eve family dinner.

Now, you have to understand my parents a bit to realize what a momentous occasion this was. My parents are Polish. They immigrated to Canada after the Second World War and took up farming in Southern Ontario. My father was a very stubborn and immovable force to reckon with. He had succeeded in farming up to a point before disaster struck and fire raged through all of his barns and a whole summer's crops, destroying everything in its wake. The cattle were all safe, but there was no feed and no barn to milk them in as winter approached. He rebuilt his barns, but he was convinced that they had to be the biggest in the land. He felt compelled to buy more cattle to fill his bigger barn, until he was facing financial ruin. In the midst of all these problems, he took to drinking heavily, and eventually he had a series of heart attacks when I was in high school. My brothers and I tried to run the farm for a few years and failed, so eventually he sold everything and moved to a small house in Brantford on a pension. He had become an alcoholic who had to be right about everything, and he wouldn't listen to anyone.

At Christmas, all of the children were expected to be in attendance for the annual Christmas Eve family fiasco—I mean supper. It was the only meal of the year where we all sat down to eat together. He would be drunk and there would usually be a fight of sorts and it was awful. I dreaded Christmas. So, this year I had a new baby, an undisciplined three and a half year old, and Denine was coming home for only two days for the first time in months; I couldn't bear to take all three of them to my parents' for the dreaded dinner, and I knew that no one would enjoy it anyway. I went to my mother's, explained everything, and invited them to come to our house. My dad had always had a weak spot in his heart for Denine, so he agreed.

Christmas with all five of us

And so for the first time that I could remember in twenty-six years, we had a beautiful Christmas Eve dinner. My whole family came and it was wonderful. My dad was almost sober and everyone had such a good time. It was the first Christmas in years where there was no arguing or fighting. Our one and only family picture with all five of us—Ken, Denine, Daniel, Melanie, and myself—was taken that night.

Two days later, Denine went back to Dr. Rygiel's. That same day, Melanie started throwing up and running a fever. Ken's mother was sick in bed with pleurisy that holiday season, so I thought that Melanie might have contracted something from her. After Melanie had been throwing up for three days, I called the doctor and had to take her to Emergency to see him. It was New Year's Eve and Ken was away with the truck. I needed to get to the hospital and I was getting frantic. After all, Melanie was only five months old. Denine had thrown up for ten days last summer and she had never recovered fully. So I called my mother-in-law and asked to borrow her new car to make the trip to town. She wouldn't let me. I had backed into a car in a parking lot six years earlier, and she still didn't trust me to drive. She said that I'd had more trouble with my three kids in five years than she'd had with her five in thirty years. I was so hurt. I had no answer to give. She said that would get up out of her sick bed and drive me to the hospital herself, but Ken arrived home a few minutes later and I was able to drive myself in the pickup truck.

I cried my heart out all the way to the city. I had had a tubal ligation after Melanie was born and there would be no more babies. I wanted to keep this one that I already had. I loved her so much and I was scared. She was throwing up clear liquids so aspirin suppositories were prescribed. They admitted her to the hospital for three days. No cause was discovered, but I was plenty scared.

Denine came home for a weekend in February. After that, because of a flu bug now and then, we kept the kids away from her. She didn't come home again.

Going to visit Denine in hospitals, and eventually at Dr. Rygiel's, was a very painful process for me. From the first time I left her until the very last, she would cry as soon as she saw me every time I visited. She would cry and cry and cry. After awhile, I'd get her settled down and she would be fine for the rest of the visit.

The visits were usually short. Daniel would get into mischief if he came along or I'd find I had something else to do. Sometimes I'd wonder what I was doing there anyway. They were taking better care of her than I could. I'd feel so helpless, so useless, and later so guilty that I didn't stay longer or go more often. And during all those visits, where was her father? He was working, of course. That was more important to him at the time. What could he do anyway? He hated hospitals. When he was a kid, his grandfather had broken a hip and spent seven years in a hospital bed and Ken's parents had taken him to visit every week. To date, Denine had been admitted into five different hospitals. She would only go to one more hospital.

Towards the end of March, I attended a Monday night meeting of the Parents' Association at Dr. Rygiel's Home for Children. I was the newcomer, and it was the only meeting I went to. The meeting was over early and I slipped upstairs to Denine's room for a final goodnight. At the time, I didn't know how final this goodbye would really be. She was still awake and I spent an unusually quiet half hour with her.

February 2, 1979

Letter from Pre-School Director, Child Development Centre

Dear Mr. and Mrs. Forster,

I understand that S. spoke to you last Friday, regarding Denine's transportation. At the moment, it is our feeling that Denine cannot be transported safely to and from the CDC. The staff at Rygiel share this concern. As a result, it was agreed that with your consent, we will temporarily discontinue Denine from attending the CDC.

We are unable to "hold" a spot for her; however, it is understood that Denine's name will be put on the top of our waiting list. In the event that safe transportation can be arranged, we would welcome Denine back into our program as soon as an opening occurs.

If you have any questions or concerns about this recommendation, do not hesitate to contact either S. or myself.

Kindest regards

Chapter 22: Dealing With Death

On Friday, the doctors at Dr. Rygiel's called to say that Denine had been taken to the hospital for a check-up, as she was having severe breathing problems. On Sunday morning, they called again before breakfast. I heard the siren wailing in the background. Before church that morning, I asked Terry to pray for her. When he prayed, something inside me broke. This was serious!

I wanted to go to the hospital to see her. We had forgotten to renew the license on our pickup truck, so I had to ask my mother-in-law to take me. She was going into Hamilton anyway with a neighbour and asked if an hour would be long enough. So, I spent just one hour at the hospital. What could I do anyway?

Denine was different this time. She did not cry when she saw me. She seemed glad to have me come. She smiled and relaxed a bit as I cuddled her to me the best I could. There were tubes everywhere and she was in an oxygen tent. I was unable to pick her, up so I just rubbed her back and smoothed her hair and told her how much I loved her. She was less rigid than other times. I stayed with her for a while, until a team of doctors I'd never seen came in and sent me out. Again I waited, and for what? They asked me more questions. They knew nothing of her history, so I had to start at the beginning. But then I had to go, because my mother-in-law was waiting for me downstairs.

That night after supper, Ken and the kids were watching TV. He tried to talk to me and couldn't get through, so he got mad and said, "Denine always did come between us."

I responded, "Do you know what I've been thinking about all day?"

"No. What?"

"Her funeral."

He paused, "So have I."

We went to bed.

I had it all planned. She would wear the long pink party dress my sister had sent her from England two years earlier. I wouldn't let them cut her hair that last week. Her hair had natural waves, like her father's. Daniel and Melanie have straight hair, just like my own.

At eleven-thirty p.m. that night, I was lying in bed reviewing the day. How was she different today from other days when I had left her? Well, she didn't cry when she first saw me. She smiled and was glad. Although she was never able to speak a word, she cried as if to say, "Why did you leave me, Mommy?"

As I lay there praying that night, I saw a vision before me as clear as anything. This is what I saw:

We were sitting in the maple rocking chair in the hospital room. Denine was on my lap as before, straddling my left leg, her twisted body turned to the left looking around at me. My left arm was encircling her shoulders straining to keep her upright. As we sat like this cuddling, she suddenly sat up, turned to face me, and called me 'Mommy'. Then, in my arms, she died.

I was suddenly confronted with the fact that my child was going to die! I prayed, *Lord, I've prayed many times before that you don't take my baby from me. This time is different. If she is indeed going to die, then I accept that as Your will.*

Such joy filled my heart and I rejoiced in God and praised Him. With this, I fell asleep. About an hour later the phone rang. Ken heard it first and ran downstairs to answer it. I waited and wondered what the call was about. Then, suddenly, I knew.

He came back upstairs and asked, "Do you know who that was?"

"Denine died," I replied.

"Yes," he said as he climbed back into bed. "They said that she suddenly went into convulsions and died. They are taking her over to General Hospital for an autopsy. It's the rules for anyone that dies within twenty four hours of admission." We would find out nearly four months later, after pestering the doctors, that the cause of death had been meningitis.

Practical Ken started talking about plans for her funeral. He wanted it private, only for the family. I protested and said something nasty to him. "You always were ashamed of her." In the end, we never did discuss her death, at least not that night. Then two weeks later, one morning before church, we had our last argument about her. I believed that she had always come between us because of the wall that Ken had built five years earlier. That wall started to tumble down now that she was Home, and I finally understood why he had shut her out. He had not wanted to get hurt again. But in the process, he had also shut me out as well as our other two children. But healing was just around the corner; it came in the form of forgiveness.

I wasn't upset or hurt or angry, but I would have to get up three times in the next hour to go to the bathroom. I called my mother in Brantford at one-thirty a.m.

"Mama."

"What is it?"

"Denine died."

"Do you want me to come?"

"Yes."

"Right now?"

"No, wait until morning."

She might just as well have come; she slept no more that night.

Ken told his dad in the barn that morning and he passed it on to his mom at breakfast time. My mother arrived around seven with my brother and they sat with me over coffee.

I called Terry, the new minister, to tell him. The poor man was on his way out the door to catch a train. He had an exam in Toronto that morning. Terry was at a complete loss for words, so he gave the phone to his wife Karen. I shared with her my vision of the night before, and she hesitated before cautiously saying that, as I spoke, she could see Denine walking up to the arms of Jesus. And as she spoke, I saw it too. She had confirmed to me what I believed. Denine was safe in the arms of Jesus. She was whole. She was no longer broken in body. God had indeed healed her. I rejoiced inward and went to face the world.

Ken's mother came over the minute she was able, when her kids went off to school. She drew me into her arms and showed me just how much she did care. I didn't cry until Wednesday afternoon, and even then, only briefly. I was too busy rejoicing inside.

We called the Marlatt Funeral Home in Dundas to handle the details. After supper, we went into Dundas to see the funeral director about the arrangements. As we were discussing the size of the casket I said, "She isn't very big."

He responded, "I know. She's downstairs."

I nearly lost my composure. She was in the building and I couldn't see her. It had not occurred to me that I could have gone to the hospital earlier. She was dead. Her spirit no longer dwelt in the crippled little body. We went over to Dr. Rygiel's, picked up a few of her things, and left the pink dress with the funeral director. I went home and started calling our family and friends. I even called my sister in England. We requested that instead of flowers, donations could be made to Dr. Rygiel's Home for Children.

Making the calls was rather interesting. Since this was the first time I was faced with such a venture, I broke all the rules. I am a nonconformist at the best of times and nobody had coached me on the proper behaviour of a mother whose child just died. I made all the calls I could think of. I called the people at Chedoke and at Dr. Rygiel's who worked with her, her doctors, etc.

To each I said much the same thing, "Denine has died and I'm so glad."

Many said, "Yes dear, it's all for the best. Now she won't suffer anymore."

They didn't understand. Yes, she had suffered a lot of pain all her short years, but this was different. They could not understand the great mercy of God who allowed her to die when I finally gave her up to Him entirely. They did not understand how God's grace was at work within me. It seemed that God had set me apart from the people I knew all my life. People had often accused me, "Why do you always have to be different? Why can't you be like everyone else?"

Tuesday morning I stepped into the doctor's office (one of the kids had a bad cold). Though the waiting room was crammed with patients, for once, I did not have to wait. They ushered us in immediately. Respect for the family of the deceased, I assume. The doctor was concerned for me and said that if I wanted anything, it was mine. He always was generous.

Not knowing the rules of behaviour, I was still rejoicing inward. I later found out that some mothers are so upset by the death of a child that they need tranquilizers to get through the funeral. God upheld me through it all. It wasn't until late that afternoon that I got to see her again, all decked out in her pretty pink party dress with a spray of pink sweetheart roses touching her cheek. I'd often thought of roses in connection with her. All the ugly wrinkles and lines of pain and suffering that had marked her face since her illness the year before were completely erased.

In life, Denine was unable to develop many fine motor skills, like blinking, laughing, and crying in one syllable. She didn't blink, but she often very deliberately closed her long dark lashes and then raised them up again when she was happy. It was a special quality that had endeared her to many. Well, as she lay there in her white casket, her eyes were closed as though she would open them in a second and a smile was beginning to curl upon her lips. She looked so beautiful, more beautiful in death than in life.

My dad and brother and two sisters were there to see her that afternoon. Amy, at sixteen, took it the hardest. She cried in my arms and I just held her. We didn't stay long. We took Daniel, who was not yet four, to see his sister one last time. He didn't understand, but he was curious. We left him and Melanie with a friend that night as we went back for the evening. Many people came to lend comfort or hope; some came purely out of curiosity. But I sat there like a queen on her throne and allowed everyone to come to me. I completely ignored Ken until I realized that none of the girls from Dr. Rygiel's or the therapists who had worked with and loved Denine for so long even knew who her father was. They had never seen him before. He had always been working. My sister sensed his isolation and abandonment and went to comfort him. I did not. I was too selfish and blind to see his hurt and need all those years.

Jeannie came after a while. She was really upset and crying uncontrollably. I took her by the arm and showed her how beautiful Denine was now. I told her how she was no longer suffering and that she was in Heaven. It was truly amazing. Jeannie had come to comfort me and God used me to comfort to her.

The next day, April 4, it turned cold and windy. Again we left the kids with the neighbour and went to the funeral. We got to sit off to the side. The rest of the family sat out front. Just before the service, I went one last time to Denine and kissed her goodbye—*until I'd see her again by and by*. A moment later, they closed the lid and I realized I'd never see her again in this life. My mother behind me sniffled and I finally broke down and cried in her arms. But I didn't cry for long. I didn't want to miss one word of this, Terry's first funeral service as our student minister. He didn't let me down. He read the message from the scripture about the sparrow, and likened Denine to a rose bud that had never opened and bloomed. I was so impressed that later I had a rose bud engraved on her stone with the words "Safe in the Arms of Jesus." I sat and listened and drank in the message of comfort and hope as a thirsty person downs a drink of refreshing water.

Four of Denine's uncles were pallbearers. We rode up the hill to Copetown at a snail's pace. Ken and I sat in the back of the chauffeur-driven limousine. It was really interesting. I viewed the whole thing like a scene in front of me; I was a bystander not a participant. We looked at each other and almost giggled. Here we were, two country bumpkins in a chauffeur-driven limousine, who would have ever predicted this? Snow started to blow around us as we drove out to the cemetery. Ken had spent the day before digging the grave for his own little girl, under a tree in the family plot. This was something he had done as a service to the community for many years. The graveside service was rushed, as a full-fledged snowstorm was raging when we got there. A quick prayer and Ken and I walked to our truck to drive home. As we walked into the wind and were covered in snow, I commented, "God is really here today. This snow shows that." The day before, we had been outside in shorts.

Almost eight inches of snow fell that afternoon. We went back to Ken's mom's house for refreshments. It was only our immediate families. The last time we had all been together was six months earlier for Melanie's baptism.

"At Denine's wake, I went to see her laying in her casket. I broke down into tears. Chris came up behind me, put her arm over my shoulders, and said, "Look how peaceful she looks now. She is no longer in pain or suffering." I turned and hugged Chris for a long time, letting my tears wash down my face. Chris's words were my biggest encouragement in getting through that time." - Jeannie

Chapter 23: "Lord Change Me"

That Saturday, I went with Terry and Karen and a couple of other ladies from our church to London, to a Women Alive conference. The guest speaker was Evelyn Christenson. She was sharing with the women there how God changes each one of us on the inside as we pray. This was the first time I had gone to a Christian gathering of this kind. I had not known that such things existed. Twenty-two hundred voices lifted in song and praise to the Lord.

The speaker, dressed in a wrinkled purple suit and snow boots, took the microphone. Her luggage had gotten separated from her at the Toronto airport and she had arrived the night before with only the clothes on her back. Her countenance was radiant, and where many women would have been in a fit of despair, she accepted this from God as one way of keeping her humble.

How can you be filled with human pride in the way you look and are dressed, when you appear on stage before 2200 women in the same suit you slept in on the plane yesterday and an old pair of boots? It was beautiful. It sure beat the stuff commercials fill our minds with on television today. Her luggage did arrive eventually and she changed to dress shoes for the afternoon program.

For the next four or five hours, Evelyn shared right from the heart about an experiment several women in her church were challenged with: to see what happens when women pray. She told us the result: that God changes us. He changes our attitudes. He changes our circumstances. He changes our lives.

I just drank it in by the hour. No one had ever told me things like this before. I had tried reading my Bible—an old King James—over the last few years. It was not easy to understand. Not having gone to Sunday school as a child, and not going to church beyond Christmas and Easter, I had not learned any of these things. And having been preoccupied with small children for the past six years, I was unable to follow along with what was being said at church, even when I went. None of it had made much sense; no one had given me any hope. My eyes could not see and my ears could not hear. But now, God had suddenly removed the veil and I was able to see and hear and understand. I cried buckets that day, overwhelmed by the love that was poured out through the people, through the singing, and through the message.

We were challenged to read Galatians chapter five and six, to read until the Lord stopped us. Then, we were to pray over the verse we had stopped at. I read and read until I came to, "Bear ye one another's burdens and so fulfil the law of Christ." All this time, we were not to speak to anyone. Can you imagine 2200 women filing down to the front of the auditorium for a carton of juice and back to their seats to read and pray without a word being spoken? Not a sound was made; it was a miracle. After lunch, we were to pair off in twos and share a burden that was on our heart. We were then to pray for the other person. I was so nervous to pray out loud for someone else to hear, but I did. And it was beautiful.

It was during the afternoon teaching that I was shown something truly remarkable. Evelyn shared a number of stories about people who had been praying for someone sick or diseased, and in each story, the person gave their loved one into God's hands.

They prayed "Not my will, Lord, but Thine." They were in fact releasing their loved one. Often, the sick person died, and they were spared any more suffering and pain. I suddenly sat up wide-eyed; that's what I had done with Denine not six days earlier! I had released her completely into the hands of God Himself, and He in His great mercy, had called her Home.

Man, was I excited now! I had had the ticket for this seminar for nearly two months. Why did it happen just five days after my girl's death? God had a message for me. His timing is always perfect. God does not make mistakes. He would not be the Almighty God if he did. He knew Denine before she was formed in my womb. He had a special plan for her life. He knew her time. He is sovereign!

Well, I was the first one out of that auditorium and the first in the autograph line to speak to Evelyn. I left tear-stains on her suit jacket and shared with her quickly what had come to pass. She knew what I was going through. She too had lost a little girl who was not perfectly formed. She had walked a mile in my shoes. How I rejoiced! God laid it on her heart to tell me that since the verse I had been given earlier was, "Bear ye one another's burdens, and so fulfil the law of Christ," (Gal. 6:2) that perhaps God had intended for me to bear the burdens of other mothers with handicapped children.

Six years later, my dearest friend Karen, had who ministered to me so much that year, gave birth to a beautiful baby girl. Her daughter, Megan, was born with multiple "congenital anomalies", which caused many complications as a result. Now she is going through the refining process. It nearly broke my heart, but I know that "all things work together for good to them that love God, to them who are the called according to his purpose." (Romans 8:28)

Chapter 24: Peace in My Heart

Life was different after Denine died. I recall feeling like I was walking a foot above the ground for several weeks after her funeral. I was still amazed at how God had so clearly spoken to me through the two visions I had the night before she died and the next morning. I felt so at peace inside. Ken was watching me very closely. He expected me to break down at some point, but it did not happen. I had peace. I was a different person on the inside.

One day, a few weeks after Denine's death, Karen had asked me point blank about my salvation. I wasn't able to talk about it. I wasn't sure what she was asking and I didn't know the language to use. So I got down on my knees by my bed one night and prayed a prayer, something like this, "God I realize that I am a sinner in need of forgiveness. I know that Jesus died on the cross to pay the penalty for my sin. I ask for forgiveness. Jesus, come into my heart." I felt nothing, so

I got up and went back to bed. In the next year, I was able to share about my experiences with Denine many times. Each time I did, it became easier. I also learned how to share my faith with others.

I started teaching at Sunday school. I took over a class of six year old boys for one Sunday and told them how Jesus had died on the cross for their sins and for mine. I was astounded at my boldness, but it had suddenly become real. Later that summer, I was again able to share the same simple plan of salvation with a group of nine year olds at Vacation Bible School.

All this time, I still said nothing to my husband. He had gotten angry the first time I tried to share the faith that was beginning to grow in my heart, so I said no more. But he was watching. I got another job selling a product at home parties and for the next year I spent many nights out late. Often, these nights were spent sharing with women who needed to know there was hope.

I was spending a lot of time with Karen. I finally had a dear friend who had time for me, who cared about what was going on in my life. It was Karen who taught me that you could have a love affair with Jesus. Karen taught me how Jesus could be a part of my family and a part of my whole life. By watching this wonderful young woman deal with everyday frustrations and problems, I learned much. Also, she gave me some life-transforming Christian books to read. One of these books was called *The Act of Marriage,* by Tim and Bev LaHaye.

I had often stated that Ken and I got married so we could have sex. Well, it was true. We got married and we had sex. We had a lot of fun in those early years. Then babies came along and it wasn't fun anymore; at least it wasn't fun for me. He would often coerce me into bed saying, "You know you want it." So we did it. But by the time I was aroused, he was done, and rolling over, he would say, "See, I told you, you wanted it." And he would go to sleep. Then I would also roll over and cry myself to sleep, again. Then God put it in my heart that there really was more to this sex thing. I found the answer in the book, *The Act of Marriage*.

What I was missing was the orgasm that should be a part of every sexual experience for women. Oh, men have orgasms all the time. It comes easy for them. But for women, it's different. It's something that needs to be learned and attained. First, we need to know it exists. Then, we need to understand how to get there. So, I set out to learn how to have an orgasm. My husband was going to learn also, except I didn't tell him what I was doing at first.

So, this is what I did. Living on the farm, he worked from home all the time and came in for meals and a nap every day. So I helped. While the kids were napping, I seduced him quickly. Just like that. Later that same night, when he was not able to do it again so quickly, we took all the time we needed to learn how to get me to that place also. And we did. Later, he told me that he was also reading the same book. Cheeky fellow. We learned to both have orgasms, and suddenly sex became exciting and fulfilling, every single time.

Chapter 25: Victory in Jesus

A year or so after Denine's death, we went on a week-long family holiday. It was our second holiday in nine years of marriage. We went with Terry and Karen and some friends and relatives of theirs, about thirty five people in all, to a resort called Linger Long Lodge. It was on an island on a lake an hour's drive north of Perry Sound. They had invited anyone at church who was interested and Ken suggested that I take the kids and go. But then Karen invited Ken specifically and we were surprised that he agreed to go.

At five, Daniel was an undisciplined, destructive entity. He was a frustrated little boy, given to constant temper tantrums, who horrified people with his words and violent behaviour. His usual greeting to people he liked was a fist in the midsection or a kick in the shins. At two, Melanie was a sweet and quiet little girl who charmed many with her loving ways. She was easy to love, and people did love her. Daniel was still bed-wetting and having dreadful nightmares almost every night. Melanie, once she was in a big bed, started having nightmares of her own. They never had them at the same time, though. Their separate night terrors would usually keep me up until three or four a.m. Ken, whose mornings usually began at five, could never understand why I was unable to bounce out of bed and get his breakfast when he came in from the barn at eight.

So we arrived at Linger Long Lodge on a Saturday afternoon, after nearly six hours on the road. At the dock, a boat was waiting to escort us to the island that was to be our home for the next six days. We carried all of our stuff up to a small one-room cabin. It had a double bed, a cot for the kids, an old refrigerator and stove, a small wood stove, a tiny counter and cupboards, and two windows. Because the cot was put in for the kids, the small table and chairs were put outside on the porch. We had most of our meals outside with the lake for a view. It rained only once.

That first evening we gathered all together in the lodge's lounge and got acquainted. We sang and worshiped God together for most of the evening. It was beautiful. My soul just drank it in. It was wonderful to stroll around the grounds throughout the day and hear people whistling or humming the tunes we'd been singing, or gathering in groups of two and three and sharing their burdens and troubles and praying one for another. One day, Karen suggested that we needed to pray for my painful back. So, several women gathered around me, sitting on the rocks beside the lake, and we prayed. One of the things I was asked to do was to recall people from my past who had hurt me or caused me pain. Names and faces came to mind as I prayed out loud and forgave the people who had bullied me. I forgave my father. When Denine's name came, with many tears, I asked her to forgive me. The pain in my back stopped.

Ken, however, was not enjoying it quite as much as I was. On Monday, he decided that he would take the kids home because they were being such a nuisance. But God had other plans for him and he decided to stay. Throughout the week we gathered as a group each morning and each evening to sing praises, and the minister who had organized all of this would teach us from the Bible. He taught on family values and Ken was listening.

No one actually told Ken that he was not saved. After all, he had gone to church all his life. He had attended Sunday school and youth group and sung in the choir. He was good, honest, and respectful. He was a man of integrity. But he had never really been faced with the decision to accept the sacrifice that Jesus Christ made when He died on the cross for his sins.

There was one lady at the retreat who was watching him and decided that he needed to "get saved." It turned out that she was an evangelist and that's what she did: she helped people understand that they needed Jesus as their saviour and prayed with them. She invited him to go out fishing in her canoe early Tuesday morning. Ken had never been in a canoe and he did not know how to swim. He was wearing a life jacket as he tried to enter the canoe, which was tied to the dock in seven feet of water. He stepped one foot in, and then tried to bring the second foot in, but he rocked the boat and, yes, the boat tipped. He fell in. She fell in. The fishing tackle fell in. As he came up for air, he noticed her coming up out of the water holding something in her hand saying, "I got it." She was holding her Bible that had fallen into the water. She had planned to take him out and help him get saved. God had another plan.

By Wednesday, Ken was totally convinced that he needed Jesus to forgive his sins. He was sitting on the steps of our cabin when he heard a voice say to him, "Go ask that man to pray with you." That man was Terry's father who had just come out of his cabin. Ken hesitated and the man went back into his cabin.

Another voice said, "You missed your chance." Ken started feeling a bit desperate and inwardly begged for another chance. Moments later, the man came outside again and Ken ran down the path to ask him to pray with him. He prayed for Ken, asking God to fill him with the Holy Spirit. Ken also prayed. He asked God to forgive his sins, and then he asked Jesus to be his saviour. So Ken believed and received, God delivered him from his sins, and he became a new creation in Jesus Christ.

"Old things are passed away; behold, all things are become new." (2 Cor. 5:17)

The next evening, after our group gathering, I took the kids back to our cabin and put them to bed. Ken decided to go back up to the lodge where many were still gathered together. He saw that they were praying for one of the teen boys, so he got closer, laid his hand on the shoulder of the nearest person, and listened. It appeared that they were praying for the boy to receive the baptism of the Holy Spirit.

Not knowing anything about this, Ken leaned in and said to God, "If there is something more, then I want that too." So he was baptised in the Holy Spirit also and received spiritual gifts. He immediately began prophesying and praying in a language that he had never learned.

Chapter 26: Life After Denine

We returned home Friday afternoon rejoicing in so great a salvation. Now we could truly become one; we could be not only one flesh, but now also one spirit. That night we began to pray for our children and for our home and farm. Within days, Daniel was healed of his bed-wetting. The nightmares stopped and I got eight hours of uninterrupted sleep. Praise God. Daniel went into the hospital for surgery a week later, and in the process they discovered and corrected a hernia that had been bothering him for years. Overnight, Daniel became a transformed child. He was getting adequate sleep now and the old pain was no longer there. His tantrums subsided. Then he entered school, and at this time, he too decided that he was sorry he was a sinner and he asked Jesus to come into his life. What a transformation. There were still a lot of wrinkles to iron out in his young life and God helped us deal with them one by one as time went along. There were too many to have them wiped out instantly. Now, after seven years, he has been moulded into a beautiful young gentleman. He still struggles with a temper and poor self-image. He struggles with reading and concepts and sticking to a job until it's done. But God has given him a gift with numbers and with sports: anything that bounces and rolls, he has to be the one to bounce it, roll it, kick it, and throw it. He is a good athlete. He also has a great sensitivity to small children.

Melanie is going on eight and is blossoming into a beautiful girl whose greatest ambition is to be a mother and to care for a baby of her own. She keeps the memory of the sister she was too young to remember alive always. At her school one day, I noticed a silhouette on the wall with the words "Who am I?" written next to it. She had written, "I have greenish eyes and yellow hair. I have a sister that died. I live on a farm." She is a grade two student who loves to read. She has so much love to give that she finds any stuffed toy or doll—pretty or homely—and just loves and cuddles it to no end.

And Ken and I, well, we have come a long, long way in these seven years since our little girl left us. We are more truly one now than ever before. We still fight, now and again. I love to have my own way too much to let things go on smoothly in perfect harmony at all times. But God has brought much healing to our lives and to our memories, and He continues to do so as we trust Him.

Do I regret taking my first-born child home from that Toronto hospital when the doctor wanted to put her away? No. I took my child home and gave her the best that I knew how. I gave her the one and only thing that she needed the most: her mother's love. Oh, children in government homes receive a lot of love. Those dedicated women and men who work in the homes and those hundreds of volunteers that give freely of their time at homes like Dr. Rygiel's, all give love to these special children. But a child's own mother has a very special love for her child, and her child knows it. My heart is broken for the many children today who do not receive that mother-love because of broken homes, divorce, or separation through placement.

Do I regret staying home that winter when I just wanted to run away from it all? If I had run away, where would I be now? Would I have the same peace and joy I have in my heart about Denine's death? My friend still regrets placing her daughter thirty years ago. My mother's friend still has Sophie at home at age thirty five. My friend Karen has her baby at home; she loves her dearly and prays for her daily through every step of her struggle and every step of her therapy.

Where would I have been through those six years if I had known and been able to trust God with every step of Denine's therapy? What would have happened if I had prayed for her daily, if I had known Him and had known how to pray specifically? I believe that God is sovereign and does not make mistakes. If He did, He would not be God. He knew the plan for my life, and slowly, He taught me to love and trust Him. He taught me to obey Him and to submit to His will. It has taken a long time—I am a very stubborn woman. But I did finally obey God by writing this book for His honour and glory, for His purpose.

Seven years have come and gone since that Sunday in April, seven long years, and yet these memories seem like only yesterday as I search back to the past and relive those sleepless nights, those high fevers, those hours of waiting in countless doctors' offices, the crying, and most of all, the pain. I was reminded of this again recently as my daughter Melanie ran a high fever and I sat up most of the night with her, trying to bring her temperature down, wrapping a wet towel around her body. God has taken us on a long journey where we have had to pass through many trials and temptations, but He also brought us triumphs. We had sickness and sorrows, but He brought us salvation. We lived through hurts and heartbreaks, but we learned to live in harmony and happiness.

It's kind of funny now, when I think about it. I have often felt that I had almost a special right or privilege to go to the head of the line. I'd be first one up to the table at picnics. I was able to use the children as an excuse, but they are not small anymore. My husband, always the gentleman, will allow everyone else to go ahead of him. I once heard someone say, "Ken's here now, there's no one else to come."

How could we be together, united as man and wife, if he can wait half of forever? Doesn't he know how I hate to wait? He is so patient. He has had to practice that patience a lot with me in all these years of marriage. God knew what He was doing when he joined us together as man and wife, until death do us part. We've been through richer and poorer—mostly poorer; I keep spending all the money as fast as Ken can earn it, sometimes faster. We've been through sickness and health. We've spent so much time dealing with sickness that we forget to be thankful for our good health. For better or worse. How much worse can things get? They can get a whole lot worse before they get better, but bad times never come to stay; they come to pass.

There is a verse in the Bible that says "Count it all joy when ye fall into divers temptations; knowing this, that the trying of your faith worketh patience. But let patience have her perfect work, that ye may be perfect and entire, wanting nothing." (James 1:2-4 NAS)

I do not handle trials well. I kick and I fight; I argue and I deny. I like to have my own way too much to submit to others and follow their suggestions. Two days after I finally started this book, I had a big argument with my husband. I sat on the stairs as he tried to work at his desk. I knew I was wrong in what I was saying. But I couldn't help feeling angry and bitter. I could not erase the jealousy and resentment that were seeking to devour my well-being. But at least I did know what I could do now. I could confess the bad feelings and leave it to God to do the rest. The quicker I am to confess my feelings of bitterness and anger and ask for forgiveness, the sooner I can get on with being normal and happy.

And the children, how do they handle Mom's tears and outbursts? One day seven year old Melanie sat me down on the couch, climbed into my lap, cuddled me lovingly and said, "It's okay, Mommy. It's gonna be okay."

God has granted me the serenity to accept the things I cannot change. He has given me the ability to change the things I can. We are still working on the wisdom to know the difference. There is too much 'self' wrapped up in my life to be perfect.

My children fight and argue. They hate to practice the piano, go to bed early, and brush their teeth. They don't like to cut the grass or help with the dishes. But then, am I any different?

Epilogue

In 1986, seven years after Denine died, I wrote our story in obedience to God who prompted me to record the events of this painful time in my life. It brought closure and it brought healing. I no longer had to carry the feelings and memories with me every day. I was set free to move on to the next stage of my life. It is also a reminder of the faith that was ***growing*** in my heart as I learned to trust Jesus Christ as my ***saviour***. It has taken me another thirty years to finally publish this book.

Some Final Thoughts

When we were discussing writing Denine's story those many years ago, Ken was given a vision.

> He saw a tiny seed start to grow
> It became a small tree
> As it grew, it became gnarled and crooked
> But it continued to grow
> The gnarled tree fell over and died
> After a while
> Seeds from the tree started to sprout up
> These new trees grew and grew
> Eventually a great forest grew
> Around this little gnarled tree
> That died

That tree was Denine and as God has allowed us to share the journey we've **had** with our profoundly handicapped child, her story lives on in the hearts of many around the world. In sharing Christ we've seen new life, hope, and healing all because of a little girl who never spoke a word.